GW01418011

The 2016 Annual Statement
Human Rights in Northern Ireland

NORTHERN
IRELAND
HUMAN
RIGHTS
COMMISSION

About us

The NI Human Rights Commission (the Commission) protects and promotes the human rights of everyone in NI. We do this by:

- keeping under review the adequacy and effectiveness in NI of law and practice relating to the protection of human rights;

- advising the Secretary of State for NI and the Executive Committee of the NI Assembly of legislative and other measures which ought to be taken to protect human rights;

- advising the NI Assembly whether proposed legislation is compatible with human rights standards;

- promoting understanding and awareness of the importance of human rights in NI by, for example, undertaking or commissioning or otherwise assisting research and educational activities.

In addition, the Commission has powers to:

- give assistance to individuals who apply to it for help in relation to proceedings involving law or practice concerning the protection of human rights;

- bring proceedings involving law or practice concerning the protection of human rights;

- institute, or intervene in, legal proceedings concerning human rights where it need not be a victim or potential victim of the unlawful act to which the proceedings relate;

- conduct investigations, and;

- require a person to provide information and documents in their possession, and to give oral evidence, in respect of an investigation;

- enter a specified place of detention in NI, in respect of an investigation, and;

- publish its advice and the outcome of its research and investigations.

Our mission statement

The Commission champions and guards the rights of all those who live in NI.

Chief Commissioner:	Les Allamby
Commissioners:	Christine Collins
	John Corey
	Milton Kerr QPM
	Grainia Long
	Alan McBride
	Marion Reynolds MBE
	Paul Yam MBE
Director:	Virginia McVea
Deputy Director:	Dr David Russell

Acronyms

CFREU	Charter of Fundamental Rights of the European Union
CAT	Convention Against Torture, Inhuman or Degrading Treatment or Punishment
CERD	Convention on the Elimination of All Forms of Racial Discrimination
CEDAW	Convention on the Elimination of Discrimination Against Women
CRC	Convention on the Rights of the Child
CRPD	Convention on the Rights of Disabled Persons
ECHR	European Convention on Human Rights
ESC	European Social Charter
FCNM	Framework Convention for the Protection of National Minorities
HRA	Human Rights Act
ICCPR	International Covenant on Civil and Political Rights
ICESCR	International Covenant on Economic, Social and Cultural Rights,
NI	Northern Ireland
UK	United Kingdom
UN	United Nations

Understanding the annual statement

The Commission's annual statement uses a traffic light system to assist readers.

Red ⬤ identifies a subject that requires immediate action by the UK Government, NI Executive or relevant public authorities and the issue may be an ongoing violation or abuse of human rights within NI.

Amber ⬤ identifies a subject that requires action by the UK Government, NI Executive or relevant public authorities. The issue may not be at a level that constitutes an ongoing violation or abuse of human rights. Initial steps toward providing an effective response could have already been taken or the necessity of taking action acknowledged by the relevant body. Such actions may have commenced but are not yet completed.

Green ⬤ identifies a subject that has been acknowledged as requiring action to protect human rights in NI and an effective response has been provided by the UK Government, NI Executive or relevant public authorities. A firm commitment to address the matter will have been demonstrated and undertaken.

Contents

The 2016 Annual Statement

Foreword

This year three UN Committees issued concluding observations on the UK's progress in implementing its treaty obligations. The reports on the CRC, ICESCR and CERD, all contain significant recommendations pertinent to NI. This reflects the effectiveness of the work of the Commission, other commissions and non-governmental organisations in highlighting NI specific human rights issues on the international stage.

Publication of the concluding observations illustrates the NI Executive's inconsistent contributions to the UK government's UN reporting duties. While the Executive played an active role in the CERD examination, no one appeared from the Executive at the equivalent examination held by the ICESCR Committee. The failure to attend means that any explanation of progress or otherwise on treaty obligations goes by default.

Finding agreement to introduce legislation to create the institutions in the Stormont House Agreement remains tantalisingly out of reach. The lack of progress in completing investigations into Troubles related deaths also remains elusive. There is a window of opportunity for dealing with outstanding legacy inquests. This requires the requisite financial resources to be made available for them to move forward with some pace.

The annual statement charts welcome progress including the placement of the Prison Ombudsman on a statutory footing, and publication of the Racial Equality Strategy. The eligibility of some gay men to give blood mirroring arrangements elsewhere in the UK and the commitment to modernise adoption law are issues that eventually moved forward following legal action.

Other issues resolved elsewhere in the UK have reached a political impasse. As a consequence, the courts have been asked to adjudicate on access to terminations of pregnancies in specific circumstances and also civil marriage for same sex couples. A resolution of these issues would be better served through the NI Assembly. Despite the progress documented in the annual statement, there remains considerable work still to be done.

The annual statement illustrates the scope of the work undertaken by the Commission over the past 12 months and is a testament to the productive and effective contribution made by the staff and commissioners in undertaking its statutory role to promote and protect the human rights of everyone in NI. I hope the analysis of where we are in 2016 is a valuable document for those interested in human rights.

Les Allamby
Chief Commissioner

Chapter 1 Introduction

The Commission was established following the Belfast (Good Friday) Agreement 1998. It is a National Human Rights Institution with 'A status' accreditation at the Global Alliance of National Human Rights Institutions.

Having assessed developments affecting human rights protections in NI throughout 2016, the Commission publishes this annual statement, operating in accordance with the NI Act 1998, and its mandate to:

- *keep under review the adequacy and effectiveness in NI of law and practice relating to the protection of human rights; and*

- *to advise the Secretary of State for NI and the Executive Committee of the NI Assembly of legislative and other measures which ought to be taken to protect human rights.*[1]

The Commission acts within the UN Paris Principles, and, in particular, the responsibility of a National Human Rights Institution to:

submit to the Government, Parliament and any other competent body, on an advisory basis either at the request of the authorities concerned or through the exercise of its power to hear a matter without higher referral, opinions, recommendations, proposals and reports on any matters concerning the promotion and protection of human rights.[2]

The Commission's assessment of developments during 2016 is premised upon the requirements of domestic human rights standards and those treaty obligations of the UN and European systems that are legally binding in NI on the basis of their ratification by the UK.

The treaties which the UK has ratified include:

- *European Convention on Human Rights (ECHR) [UK ratification 1951] – given further domestic effect by the Human Rights Act (HRA) 1998;*

- *European Social Charter (ESC) [UK ratification 1962];*

- *Framework Convention for the Protection of National Minorities (FCNM) [UK ratification 1998];*

- *Convention on Action against Trafficking in Human Beings [UK ratification 2008];*

- *European Charter for Regional or Minority Languages [UK ratification 2001];*

- *International Covenant on Civil and Political Rights (ICCPR) [UK ratification 1976];*

- *International Covenant on Economic, Social and Cultural Rights, (ICESCR) [UK ratification 1976];*

- *Convention on the Elimination of All Forms of Racial Discrimination (CERD) [UK ratification 1969];*

- *Convention on the Elimination of Discrimination Against Women, (CEDAW) [UK ratification 1986];*

---

1   See section 69, NI Act 1998.
2   Principles relating to the Status of National Institutions, adopted by UN General Assembly resolution 48/134 of 20 December 1993

- *Convention on the Rights of the Child (CRC) [UK ratification 1991];*

- *Optional Protocol to the Convention on the Rights of the Child on the Involvement of Children in Armed Conflict [UK ratification 2003]*

- *Optional Protocol to the Convention on the Rights of the Child on the Sale of Children, Child Prostitution and Child Pornography [UK ratification 2009]*

- *Convention Against Torture, Inhuman or Degrading Treatment or Punishment (CAT) [UK ratification 1988];*

- *the UN Educational, Scientific and Cultural Organisation Convention on the Protection and Promotion of the Diversity of Cultural Expressions [UK ratification 2007]*

- *Charter of Fundamental Rights of the European Union (CFREU) [UK ratification 2000]*

- *Convention on the Rights of Disabled Persons, (CRPD) [UK ratification 2009].*

Under the NI Act 1998, section 24 (1) Ministers of the Executive Committee of the NI Assembly (NI Executive) and Executive departments are required to ensure that all legislation and actions are compatible with the ECHR.[3]

The NI Act 1998, section 26, requires compliance with other international human rights obligations, and that for this purpose the Secretary of State for NI may, by direct order, prevent any proposed action by Ministers of the NI Executive and devolved Executive departments.[4]

The ECHR is given further domestic effect in the UK as a consequence of the HRA. Subject to section 6 (3), all public authorities in NI must ensure that their actions are compatible with the HRA. The definition of a public authority includes a 'court or tribunal, and any person certain of whose functions are functions of a public nature'.[5] This means that private sector contractors may, at times, be subject to the requirements of the HRA. Government departments have the duty to ensure that actions carried out following public procurement exercises comply with the ECHR.

The Commission, in assessing compliance with international human rights standards, takes account of the findings of the international monitoring bodies that are directed to or otherwise apply to NI, as well as the general comments and other interpretive texts adopted by such bodies.

---

3 Section 24 of the NI Act 1998 states: 'A Minister or NI department has no power to make, confirm or approve any subordinate legislation, or to do any act, so far as the legislation or act— (a) is incompatible with any of the Convention rights'

4 Section 26 of the NI Act 1998 states: 'If the Secretary of State considers that any action proposed to be taken by a Minister or NI department would be incompatible with any international obligations, with the interests of defence or national security or with the protection of public safety or public order, he may by order direct that the proposed action shall not be taken'

5 See section 6, Human Rights Act 1998

Treaty examinations and reports issued in 2016:

UN Convention on the Rights of the Child

The UN CRC Committee examined the UK's fifth periodic report on compliance with the UN CRC in 2016. The Committee published its concluding observations in May 2016.

International Covenant on Economic Social and Cultural Rights

The UN ICESCR Committee examined the UK's sixth periodic report on compliance with the ICESCR in 2016. The Committee published its concluding observations in June 2016.

UN Convention on the Elimination of Racial Discrimination

The UN CERD Committee examined the UK's twenty-first to twenty-third periodic reports on compliance with the ICERD in 2016. The Committee published its concluding observations in July 2016.

European Commission against Racism and Intolerance

In June 2016 the European Commission against Racism and Intolerance adopted findings and recommendations relating to the UK as part of its fifth monitoring cycle.

All of the above reports contained recommendations and findings of both specific and general relevance to NI. These reports, recommendations and findings are set out in the relevant sections of the annual statement.

Chapter 2 Substantive rights and issues

Equality and non-discrimination

ICCPR	Article 2(1) Article 3 Article 24 Article 2
CRC	
ECHR	Article 14
CFREU	Article 20 Article 21 Article 23
CRPD	
ICESCR	Article 2(2) Article 3
CERD	
CEDAW	
FCNM	

Consolidating, strengthening and clarifying equality protections

Three UN treaty bodies have raised concerns that NI law does not provide for a single legislative instrument to consolidate, clarify and enhance existing equality protections.[6] In NI discrimination is prohibited by a number of laws and regulations, resulting in a complex framework.[7] The Commission has again reported the matter to the UN in 2016.[8] The UN ICESCR Committee subsequently stated its regret that, despite its previous recommendation the situation in NI has not been addressed. It urged, 'a similar level of protection to rights holders with regard to all grounds of discrimination for all individuals in all jurisdictions of the State party, including NI'.[9]

---

6   UN Committee on Economic, Social and Cultural Rights, Concluding observations on the sixth periodic report of the United Kingdom of Great Britain and Northern Ireland E/C.12/GBR/CO/6, UN Economic and Social Council, 14 July 2016, para 23; UN Committee on the Elimination of Racial Discrimination, Concluding observations on the twenty-first to twenty-third periodic reports of United Kingdom, CERD/C/GBR/CO/21-23, UN CERD, 26 August 2016, para 8 (c); UN Committee on the Elimination of Discrimination Against Women, Concluding observations on the seventh periodic report of the United Kingdom of Great Britain and Northern Ireland, CEDAW/C/GBR/CO/7, UN CEDAW, July 2013, para 18.

7   See, Employment Equality (Age) Regulations (NI) 2006; Disability Discrimination Act 1995; Special Educational Needs & Disability (NI) Order 2005; Equal Pay Act (NI) 1970; Sex Discrimination (NI) Order 1976; Race Relations (NI) Order 1997; Fair Employment & Treatment (NI) Order 1998; Employment Equality (Sexual Orientation) Regulations (NI) 2003; Equality Act (Sexual Orientation) Regulations (NI) 2006; and, Northern Ireland Act 1998.

8   NIHRC, Submission to the UN Committee on Economic, Social and Cultural Rights 58th Session on the Sixth Periodic Report of the United Kingdom's Compliance with ICESCR, April 2016, p. 25.

9   UN Committee on Economic, Social and Cultural Rights, Concluding observations on the sixth periodic report of the United Kingdom of Great Britain and Northern Ireland E/C.12/GBR/CO/6, UN Economic and Social Council, 14 July 2016, para 24.

The Commission has also raised particular concern about the legislative framework protecting against racial discrimination to the UN CERD Committee, noting less protection on the grounds of colour and nationality.[10] In 2016, the Committee recommended that the State Party, 'ensure that the authorities of NI act without further delay to adopt comprehensive legislation prohibiting racial discrimination in accordance with the provisions of the Convention'.[11]

Following a country visit, the European Commission against Racism and Intolerance raised concerns about the lack of protection from discrimination on the grounds of gender identity, recommending that legislation is enacted.[12] European Commission against Racism and Intolerance also recommended, as a priority for implementation, that the authorities 'consolidate equality legislation into a single, comprehensive equality act, taking inspiration from the Equality Act 2010, and taking account of the recommendations of the Equality Commission for NI'.[13]

The Commission notes that the NI Executive previously expressed its intent to review the current equality framework through a step-by-step approach rather than through a single legislative instrument.[14] However the Junior Minister, Alistair Ross stated in October 2016 in an Assembly debate on the Racial Equality Strategy that:

The Statute Book is an incredibly messy thing. There could be piecemeal approaches taken to different legislation that could be encompassed in a consolidated Bill of some sort. That is something that the Executive Office will look at. We are going to examine the statute book to see what legislation is there. If a consolidation Bill is required, that can be something we will give consideration to.[15]

The Commission continues to advise on the need to strengthen, simplify and harmonise equality legislation within a single equality act.[16]

Age discrimination

There is currently no prohibition on discrimination in the provision of goods, facilities and services in NI on the basis of age. The Office of the First Minister and Deputy First Minster (now the Executive Office) published a consultation document in 2015 proposing to extend age discrimination legislation to cover the provision of goods, facilities and services.[17] The Commission welcomed the initiative but, along with the NI Commissioner for Children and Young People and a number of children's organisations, expressed concern that these proposals exclude children under 16.[18] NI Executive Ministers have stated that the decision to exclude under 16s was made on the basis of seeking to advance legislation as quickly as possible with the aim of eventually extending age discrimination

10   NIHRC, Submission to the United Nations Committee on the Elimination of Racial Discrimination: Parallel Report on the 21st to 23rd Periodic Reports of the United Kingdom under the International Convention on the Elimination of All forms of Racial Discrimination, July 2016, para 44.

11   UN Committee on the Elimination of Racial Discrimination, Concluding observations on the twenty-first to twenty-third periodic reports of United Kingdom, CERD/C/GBR/CO/21-23, UN CERD, 26 August 2016, para 8 (c).

12   European Commission against Racism and Intolerance, Report on the United Kingdom (fifth monitoring cycle), CRI(2016)38, Adopted on 29 June 2016, European Commission against Racism and Intolerance, 4 October 2016, para 143.

13   European Commission against Racism and Intolerance, Report on the United Kingdom (fifth monitoring cycle), CRI(2016)38, Adopted on 29 June 2016, European Commission against Racism and Intolerance, 4 October 2016, para 22.

14   See comments to the UN Committee on the Elimination of Discrimination against Women, Replies of United Kingdom of Great Britain and Northern Ireland to the list of issues to be taken up in connection with the consideration of its seventh periodic report, CEDAW/C/GBR/Q/7/Add.1, UN CEDAW, February 2013, para 17; See also comments in the draft Racial Equality Strategy, OFMDFM,' A Sense of Belonging: Delivering Social Change through a Racial Equality Strategy for Northern Ireland 2014 – 2024' (pp. 38 and 40), consultation period August – October 2014.

15   Northern Ireland Assembly, Official Report (Hansard) Tuesday 11 October 2016, Vol 116, No. 4, p. 14.

16   NIHRC, Human Rights Priorities for the 2016 Programme for Government, July 2016, p. 6.

17   OFMDFM, Proposals to Extend Age Discrimination Legislation (Age Goods, Facilities and Services) Consultation Document, July 2015.

18   NI Commissioner for Children and Young People, 'Don't exclude us! Strengthening protection for Children and Young people when Accessing Goods, Facilities and Services', 2013; Northern Ireland NGO Alternative Report, Submission to the United Nations Committee on the Rights of the Child for Consideration During the Committee's Examination of the United Kingdom of Great Britain and Northern Ireland Government Report, Children's Law Centre and Save the Children NI, June 2015, p. 14; NIHRC, Response to consultation on Proposals to Extend Age Discrimination Legislation (Age Goods, Facilities and Services), 2015.

protection to children under 16.[19] The legislation was not progressed during the mandate of the previous NI Assembly.[20]

In June 2016 the UN CRC Committee recommended that the State Party including the NI Executive:

Consider the possibility of expanding legislation to provide protection of all children under 18 years of age against discrimination on the grounds of their age.[21]

Eligibility to donate blood

In its 2015 annual statement the Commission raised concerns regarding the imposition of a lifetime ban in NI on blood donations from men who have sex with other men.[22]

In June 2016 the Health Minister, Michelle O'Neill announced that the policy of permanent deferral applying to men who have sex with other men would be replaced by a temporary 12 month deferral period.[23] The new deferral system took effect on 1 September 2016.[24] This brought NI into line with the rest of the UK. The new system permits gay and bisexual men to give blood one year after their last sexual contact with another man. This requirement applies to all gay and bisexual men, including healthy gay and bisexual men in monogamous relationships.

Extension of civil marriage to same sex couples

The UN Human Rights Committee has welcomed the adoption of the Marriage (Same Sex Couples) Act 2013, which provides for same sex marriage in England and Wales.[25] Similar provision was made in Scotland through the Marriage and Civil Partnership (Scotland) Act 2014.[26] A year later, following a referendum, Ireland also enacted the Constitution (Marriage Equality) Act 2015 to provide for same sex marriage.[27]

There have been a number of legislative initiatives in the NI Assembly aimed at extending civil marriage to same sex couples. In October 2015 the NI Assembly debated a motion calling on the NI Executive to table legislation to allow for same-sex marriage. Whilst a majority of members of the NI Assembly voted for this motion it did not pass as a petition of concern was lodged requiring that the motion be passed on a cross community basis.[28]

The Minister of Finance, Maírtín Ó Muilleoír, has indicated his intention to introduce a Bill providing for same sex marriage in NI, stating:

I am committed to the concept of equal marriage and I want this Assembly to legislate for such marriage as soon as possible… but we have a little way to go in terms of bringing other Members with us and securing the necessary support from the floor. I believe we will be able to do that during this mandate and that Members will choose to legislate, rather than be forced to legislate on foot of an adverse judgment. We must do the groundwork now, so that, as soon as the Executive and the Assembly signal their readiness, we are able to move swiftly toward

19   Committee for the Office of the First Minister and Deputy First Minister, 'Age Discrimination Legislation: OFMDFM Junior Ministers and Officials', OFFICIAL REPORT (Hansard), 15 April 2015.

20   AQO 9721/11-16, tabled by Mr Samuel Gardiner MLA, 18 February 2016

21   UN Committee on the Rights of the Child, Concluding Observations on the Fifth Periodic Report of the United Kingdom of Great Britain and NI, CRC/C/GBR/CO/5, UN CRC, 12 July 2016.

22   NIHRC, Submission to the United Nations' Committee on Economic, Social and Cultural Rights, Parallel Report on the Sixth Periodic Report of the United Kingdom under the International Covenant on Economic, Social and Cultural Rights, September 2015, p. 59.

23   Department of Health, 'Health Minister Michelle O'Neill lifts lifetime ban on blood donation,' 02 June 2016.

24   BBC News, 'Gay blood donations: Lifetime ban in NI on gay men donating blood lifted', 1 September 2016.

25   UN Human Rights Committee, Concluding observations on the seventh periodic report of the United Kingdom of Great Britain and Northern Ireland, CCPR/C/GBR/CO/7, UN HRC, July 2015, para 3.

26   Same Sex and Civil Partnership (Scotland) Act 2014.

27   Thirty-fourth Amendment of the Constitution (Marriage Equality) Act 2015.

28   NIA Official Report: Monday 02 November 2015. Private Members business: Marriage Equality.

introduction. I have, therefore, asked my officials to start working on a draft Bill and to initiate discussions with other interested Departments, given that the Bill may touch on matters that are not within my Department's remit.[29]

The First Minister has indicated that the Democratic Unionist Party will continue to use the petition of concern mechanism as a means to block any legislative change in respect of introducing same sex marriage for the rest of the five year mandate.[30]

A same sex couple has challenged the unavailability of same sex marriages in NI in the High Court, while a same sex couple who had been married elsewhere in the UK sought to have their marriage recognised in NI through a High Court challenge. A decision is awaited on the cases which were heard together.

Gender equality strategy

The Office of the First Minister and Deputy First Minister (now the Executive Office) Gender Equality Strategy 2006-2016 is the policy framework under which the NI Executive promotes gender equality in NI. Responsibility for the Gender Equality Strategy now lies with the Department for Communities. Between 2008 and 2011, the strategy was complemented by two cross-departmental action plans, one for women and one for men. In 2013, a 'midterm review' of the strategy considered that while its vision, objectives and key actions were still relevant, 'progress against it had been limited and implementation and monitoring could be improved'.[31] Among many conclusions, the review noted that, '[o]utcomes and targets in the action plans were generally not SMART (Specific, Measureable, Achievable, Realistic and Time-bound) and … this made it difficult to judge if a target or outcome had been achieved'.[32] The review gave an indicative achievement rate of 29 per cent of the action points across all departments.[33]

The Commission understands that the Gender Equality Unit is pursuing a process of 'co-design' for the Strategy and consulted with the Gender Advisory Panel and the ad hoc Women's Policy Group (a NGO collaboration) on a draft of the new Gender Equality Strategy in June 2015. The Commission has called for the publication of a draft NI Gender Equality Strategy for public consultation. At the time of writing, no public consultation has taken place. The First Minister indicated in a response to an Assembly question that the new strategy would be published in late 2016.[34] The 2006-2016 strategy will remain in place until the new strategy is developed and operational.[35] The Commission raised the issue of the outstanding strategy with the UN ICESCR Committee in 2016.[36]

Hate crimes

In 2015, the UN Human Rights Committee recommended that the UK, including the NI Executive, seek to eradicate racism through:

(a) Effectively implementing and enforcing the existing relevant legal and policy frameworks on combating hate crimes;

(b) Introducing new awareness-raising campaigns aimed at promoting respect for human rights and tolerance for diversity;

---

29   AQO 82/16-21, tabled by Mr Maírtín Ó Muilleoír MLA, 20 June 2016.

30   BBC, Same-sex marriage: Arlene Foster criticised for 'childish' online abuse comments, 28 October 2016.

31   OFMDFM/NISRA, Gender Equality Strategy 2006-2016 Review, April 2013, para 2.2 (see also para 2.1).

32   OFMDFM/NISRA, Gender Equality Strategy 2006-2016 Review, April 2013, para 2.6.

33   OFMDFM/NISRA, Gender Equality Strategy 2006-2016 Review, April 2013, para 4.16.

34   AQT 3603 11-16, Ms Bronwyn Mc Gahan 7 March 2016

35   AQO 9133/11-16, tabled by Mr Danny Kennedy, 12 November 2015

36   NIHRC, Submission to the UN Committee on Economic, Social and Cultural Rights 58th Session on the Sixth Periodic Report of the United Kingdom's Compliance with ICESCR, April 2016, Paras 12.1-12.4.

(c) Improving the reporting of cases of incitement to discrimination, hostility or violence, and of hate crimes;

(d)Thoroughly investigating alleged cases of incitement to discrimination, hostility or violence, and hate crimes, prosecuting perpetrators and, if convicted, punishing them with appropriate sanctions, and providing victims with adequate remedies, including compensation. [37]

The Police Service NI has reported 1,221 racist incidents and 853 racist crimes in the financial year 2015/16, a decrease on the previous year, with 135 fewer incidents and 67 fewer crimes recorded.[38]

The tool for prosecuting the hate element of a crime in NI is the Criminal Justice (No. 2) (NI) Order 2004, often called the 'aggravated by hostility' sentencing legislation. This legislation is applied in conjunction with a base offence, such as criminal damage or assault, and allows the courts to impose an enhanced sentence.[39] It covers hostility based on the grounds of race, religion, disability and sexual orientation and requires judges to 'state in open court that the offence was so aggravated'.[40] The Commission raised concerns with the UN CERD Committee that the legislation does not cover a sectarian motivation, meaning that a crime must fall under race or religion in order for the courts to be able to impose an enhanced sentence. In 2016, the European Commission against Racism and Intolerance also recommended that this legislation be extended to cover gender identity.[41]

The Public Prosecution Service NI publishes statistics on cases considered by a prosecutor to have been 'aggravated by hostility'. For the first time in 2015, these statistics included whether or not the judge accepted the 'aggravated by hostility' element and imposed an enhanced sentence. For the period 2014/15, 13 of 46 defendants convicted (28 per cent) in the Crown Court received an enhanced sentence where the Judge accepted that the aggravating feature of the offence(s) had been proven beyond reasonable doubt.[42] In the Youth and Magistrates Courts this figure was 40 out of 195 defendants convicted (21 per cent).[43] In 2015/16, only one out of 14 defendants convicted in the Crown Court received an enhanced sentence on the basis that the hostility element was proven.[44] In the Youth and Magistrates Courts 88 out of 244 defendants convicted received an enhanced sentence (36 per cent).[45]

As reported in previous annual statements, the Commission has published an investigation report 'Racist hate crime: human rights and the criminal justice system in NI'.[46] The NI Policing Board has been carrying out a human rights thematic review on how the Police Service for NI is addressing hate crime.[47] In addition, the Criminal Justice Inspectorate NI has been conducting an inspection of the Criminal Justice Response to Hate Crimes. Both initiatives are due to be published shortly.

37   UN Human Rights Committee, Concluding observations on the seventh periodic report of the United Kingdom of Great Britain and Northern Ireland, CCPR/C/GBR/CO/7, UN HRC, July 2015, para 10.

38   Incidents and Crimes with a Hate Motivation Recorded by the Police in Northern Ireland: Quarterly Update to 31 March 2016 (Providing final figures for 1st April 2015 to 31st March 2016), PSNI, 12 May 2016, see Table 1.

39   NIHRC, Submission to the United Nations Committee on the Elimination of Racial Discrimination: Parallel Report on the 21st to 23rd Periodic Reports of the United Kingdom under the International Convention on the Elimination of All forms of Racial Discrimination, July 2016, para 134.

40   The Criminal Justice (No. 2) (NI) Order 2004, Article 2.

41   European Commission against Racism and Intolerance, Report on the United Kingdom (fifth monitoring cycle), CRI(2016)38, Adopted on 29 June 2016, European Commission against Racism and Intolerance, 4 October 2016, paras 139 and 141.

42   Public Prosecution Service for Northern Ireland, Statistical Bulletin: Cases Involving Hate Crime 2014/15, 30 July 2015, p.16.

43   Public Prosecution Service for Northern Ireland, Statistical Bulletin: Cases Involving Hate Crime 2014/15, 30 July 2015, p.16.

44   Public Prosecution Service for Northern Ireland , Statistical Bulletin: Cases Involving Hate Crime 2015/16 1 April 2015 to 31 March 2016, August 2016, p.17.

45   Public Prosecution Service for Northern Ireland , Statistical Bulletin: Cases Involving Hate Crime 2015/16 1 April 2015 to 31 March 2016, August 2016, p.17.

46   NIHRC, 'Aggravated by Racial Hostility: Human rights and the criminal justice system', Belfast 2013.

47   Policing Board NI, 'Policing of Race Hate Crime under review', 20 November 2015.

Intersectional multiple discrimination

NI legislation does not recognise intersectional multiple discrimination cases.[48] The Equality Act 2010 which covers other parts of the UK contains a dual discrimination provision, however this has not been brought into force as of yet, despite a recommendation from the House of Lords Select Committee on the Equality Act 2010 and Disability on the issue.[49] At present, each discrimination ground has to be considered and ruled on separately. The Equality Commission NI reports 'clear evidence' that individuals in NI experience multiple discrimination.[50] For example, over a twelve month period during 2015/16, the Equality Commission NI received 107 hybrid 'race' discrimination enquiries/applications.[51]

The Commission has raised the matter with a number of treaty bodies in 2016.[52] There is however no commitment from the NI Executive to introduce legislation providing for intersectional multiple discrimination claims in NI.[53] The Commission continues to call for the prohibition of intersectional discrimination through a single equality act.

Persons with disabilities

In May 2015, the then Junior Ministers Michelle McIlveen and Jennifer McCann announced that the NI Executive's 'Strategy to Improve the Lives of People with Disabilities 2012 – 2015' would be extended until March 2017.[54] This extension had been anticipated as many of the actions proposed by the strategy had not been implemented. The first annual report on the strategy was published in 2015.[55]

Within the Office of the First Minister and Deputy First Minister (now the Executive Office) annual report on the Disability Strategy a commitment was made to the establishment of:

an oversight group to drive forward and monitor the implementation of the strategy. This group will be comprised of key stakeholders from the statutory, voluntary and academic sectors as well as individuals with disabilities. The group will also assist with monitoring and reporting against the UN CRPD more generally.[56]

Throughout 2016 this commitment has not been realised and the absence of independent oversight has potentially contributed to the lack of activity around the implementation of the actions within the strategy. Responsibility for disability was transferred to the newly formed Department for Communities in 2016. The Commission has met with key officials emphasising the need to prioritise implementation of the strategy.

---

48   'Intersectional discrimination' refers to a discriminatory experience based on two or more grounds taken together, but where each ground could not prove the discrimination if taken individually.

49   Select Committee on the Equality Act 2010 and Disability, "The Equality Act 2010: The Impact on Disabled People", Report of session 2015-16, HL Paper 117, published 24 March 2016.

50   Equality Commission for Northern Ireland, Recommendations for law reform: Strengthening protection against racial discrimination, August 2014, pp. 33-38.

51   Equality Commission for Northern Ireland, Annual Report 2015/16, July 2016, p. 20.

52   NIHRC, Submission to the UN Committee on Economic, Social and Cultural Rights 58th Session on the Sixth Periodic Report of the United Kingdom's Compliance with ICESCR, April 2016, Paras 9.1-9.3; NIHRC, Submission to the United Nations Committee on the Elimination of Racial Discrimination: Parallel Report on the 21st to 23rd Periodic Reports of the United Kingdom under the International Convention on the Elimination of All forms of Racial Discrimination, July 2016, Paras 44-48; NIHRC, Submission to the Advisory Committee on the Framework Convention for the Protection of National Minorities: Parallel Report to the Advisory Committee on the Fourth Monitoring Report of the UK, 2016, Paras 49-52.

53   The Commission notes that the UK Government has not brought into force a narrowly drafted provision within the Equality Act 2010 permitting dual discrimination cases elsewhere in the UK. The Equality Act 2010, Section 14 (applicable in GB only) includes provision for dual discrimination cases limited to direct discrimination claims only but this provision has never been brought into force.

54   OFMDFM, Junior Ministers Jennifer McCann and Michelle McIlveen have announced the Executive's Disability Strategy will be extended until the end of March 2017, 12 May 2015.

55   NI Executive, 'A Strategy to improve the lives of people with disabilities 2012-2015' Annual Report, June 2015.

56   NI Executive, 'A Strategy to improve the lives of people with disabilities 2012-2015' Annual Report, June 2015. p. 28.

Racial equality strategy

The Racial Equality Strategy 2015 – 2025 was published in December 2015, which has been welcomed by the UN CERD Committee in its 2016 concluding observations.[57] The strategy established a Racial Equality Subgroup which hosted its first meeting in September 2016. The Commission sits on the subgroup in an advisory capacity. A detailed and action oriented plan remains outstanding and this has been raised through the Racial Equality Subgroup.

A number of thematic groups are proposed, including one on Immigration and one on Roma, Gypsies and Travellers. Both the UN CERD Committee and the European Commission against Racism and Intolerance have raised concerns about the lack of a comprehensive strategy for Roma, Gypsy and Travellers. In 2016, the UN CERD Committee recommended the development of, 'a comprehensive strategy, in consultation with members of Gypsies, Traveller and Roma communities, to ensure a systematic and coherent approach in addressing the challenges that they continue to face in the fields of health, education, housing and employment, and ensure its effective implementation by adopting specific action plans and effective oversight and monitoring mechanisms to track progress, with adequate human and financial resources'.[58] The European Commission against Racism and Intolerance made similar recommendations.[59]

Religious tolerance

In February 2015, Paul Givan MLA proposed the Freedom of Conscience Amendment Bill. The Commission's advice on this Bill, was that it was incompatible with the ECHR as a commercial business cannot discriminate against a person on the grounds of their sexual orientation.[60] The Supreme Court affirmed that such discrimination was unlawful regardless of the business owner's religious beliefs in the 2013 case of Bull v Hall.[61] The Freedom of Conscience Amendment Bill was therefore outside the legislative competence of the NI Assembly. The Bill was not introduced to the NI Assembly during the last mandate.

Nevertheless, the issue of religious tolerance has remained live in NI with the case of Lee v Ashers Baking Co Ltd. The Equality Commission NI assisted Gareth Lee in taking legal action against Ashers Baking Company, after the company refused to provide him with a cake with the slogan 'Support Gay Marriage' in May 2014. In their evidence to the County Court, the Defendants stated that they could not provide Gareth Lee with the cake as it was contrary to their religious beliefs. In her judgment, District Judge Brownlie found that Ashers Baking Company had unlawfully discriminated against Mr Lee on the grounds of his sexual orientation, contrary to regulation 5[1] of the Equality Act (Sexual Orientation) Regulations (NI) 2006.[62] The Court also ruled that Ashers had directly discriminated against Mr Lee on the grounds of his religious beliefs/political opinion contrary to Article 3(2) of the Fair Employment and Treatment Order 1998.[63] District Judge Brownlie further affirmed that the law requires businesses to supply their services to all. The District Judge noted that Ashers Baking Company were not a religious organisation but were conducting their business for profit; there were therefore no exceptions to the 2006 regulations in these circumstances.

57   UN Committee on the Elimination of Racial Discrimination, Concluding observations on the twenty-first to twenty-third periodic reports of United Kingdom, CERD/C/GBR/CO/21-23, UN CERD, 26 August 2016.

58   UN Committee on the Elimination of Racial Discrimination, Concluding observations on the twenty-first to twenty-third periodic reports of United Kingdom, CERD/C/GBR/CO/21-23, UN CERD, 26 August 2016, para 25 (a).

59   European Commission against Racism and Intolerance, Report on the United Kingdom (fifth monitoring cycle), CRI(2016)38, Adopted on 29 June 2016, European Commission against Racism and Intolerance, 4 October 2016, para 109.

60   NIHRC, 'Consultation on the Northern Ireland Freedom of Conscience Amendment Bill' 2015

61   The Supreme Court of the United Kingdom, Bull and another (Appellants) v Hall and another [2013] UKSC 73, 27 November 2013

62   District Judge Brownlie, Gareth Lee v. Ashers Baking Company Ltd & Colin McArthur and Karen McArthur [2015] NICty 2, NI Courts and Tribunal Service, 19 May 2015.

63   The Fair Employment and Treatment (Northern Ireland) Order 1998, Statutory Instruments, 16 December 1998.

In early 2016, Ashers appealed the ruling to the Court of Appeal. In March 2016 the Attorney General of NI intervened in the case querying the legality of the 2006 Regulations in their application to those with religious belief. The Appeal case was heard in June 2016 and judgment was given in October 2016. In their judgment, the Court of Appeal unanimously upheld the District Judge's ruling that Mr Lee had been directly discriminated against on the grounds of his sexual orientation.[64] The Lord Justices of Appeal also ruled that the 2006 regulations did not discriminate against the appellants as the legislation treated all parties in the same way. The Court also ruled that the 2006 regulations were lawfully made and did not discriminate against the appellants as the legislation treated all parties in the same way. The Court noted that the answer, in this case, was not to remove the equality protections in the 2006 regulations, but rather, 'for the supplier of services to cease distinguishing, on prohibited grounds, between those who may or may not receive the service'.[65] The Court of Appeal also did not find any breach of the appellant's Article 9 ECHR right to manifest their religion or Article 10 ECHR right to freedom of expression.

Sectarianism

The Police Service NI has reported 1352 sectarian incidents and 1001 sectarian crimes in the financial year 2015/16 a decrease on the previous year, with 165 fewer incidents and 42 fewer crimes recorded.[66] The continuance of sectarian violence raises significant human rights concerns, including: individuals being subjected to torture, inhuman and degrading treatment; individuals being forced from their homes and denied the right to choose their place of residence; and individuals being denied the right to express their culture.

Throughout 2016, flags, cultural symbols and emblems remained a source of dispute. The Stormont House Agreement proposed the establishment of a Commission on Flags, Identity, Culture and Tradition. This was to be established by June 2015 and produce a report within 18 months.[67] The membership of the Commission on Flags, Identity, Culture and Tradition was announced in June 2016.[68] It has now commenced its work.

The 'Together Building a United Community' strategy contains a commitment to develop a statutory definition of 'sectarianism' and 'good relations'. No proposals for law reform have been published in 2016.[69]

In August 2016, the UN CERD Committee reiterated its, 'previous concern that measures to tackle racism and sectarianism are kept outside the framework of protections against discrimination provided by the Convention and the Durban Programme of Action'[70] and recommended that the next periodic report contain information on concrete measures adopted to address racial discrimination and on the impact of the Together: Building a United Community Strategy.[71]

---

64   Court of Appeal of Northern Ireland, Gareth Lee v. Colin McArthur, Karen McArthur and Ashers Baking Company Limited 2016 NICA 39, NI Courts and Tribunal Service, 24 October 2016.

65   Court of Appeal of Northern Ireland, Gareth Lee v. Colin McArthur, Karen McArthur and Ashers Baking Company Limited 2016 NICA 39, NI Courts and Tribunal Service, 24 October 2016, para 100.

66   PSNI, Incidents and Crimes with a Hate Motivation Recorded by the Police in Northern Ireland: Quarterly Update to 31 March 2016, (Providing final figures for 1st April 2015 to 31st March 2016) Published 12 May 2016, see Figure 10. Table 13 and Table 14 indicate that in 2014/15 there were a total of 1,517 total number of sectarian incidents and 1,043 sectarian crimes recorded by the PSNI.

67   The Stormont House Agreement, 2014, p. 4.

68   NI Executive, 'Foster and McGuinness announce membership of the Commission on Flags, Identity, Culture and Tradition', 20 June 2016.

69   OFMDFM Committee Report on the Inquiry into Building a United Community Reference: NIA 257/11-16.

70   UN Committee on the Elimination of Racial Discrimination, Concluding observations on the twenty-first to twenty-third periodic reports of United Kingdom, CERD/C/GBR/CO/21-23, UN CERD, 26 August 2016, para 36.

71   UN Committee on the Elimination of Racial Discrimination, Concluding observations on the twenty-first to twenty-third periodic reports of United Kingdom, CERD/C/GBR/CO/21-23, UN CERD, 26 August 2016, para 37.

🟠 Sexual Orientation Strategy

Office of the First Minister and Deputy First Minister (now the Executive Office) issued a public consultation in March 2014 on the development of a Sexual Orientation Strategy.[72] Phase one of the consultation, which included information gathering and seeking views on the content of the strategy, has completed. Responsibility for gender equality and sexual orientation has transferred to the Department of Communities. The Department for Communities are currently considering how to take this forward in the context of the NI Executive's draft Social Strategy. This will be issued for consultation but has not yet been published.[73]

---

72   OFMDFM, Developing a Sexual Orientation Strategy - Consultation document and Questionnaire, March 2014.

73   Correspondence from Department for Communities to Commons, 15 November 2016.

Right to life

ICCPR	Article 6
ECHR	Article 2
CRFEU	Article 2
CRC	Article 6(1)
CRPD	Article 10

Conflict related deaths: transitional justice and individual cases

In 2015, the UN Human Rights Committee again focused its attention on NI, recommending that the UK, including the NI Executive:

(a) Ensure, as a matter of particular urgency, that independent, impartial, prompt and effective investigations, including those proposed under the Stormont House Agreement, are conducted to ensure a full, transparent and credible account of the circumstances surrounding events in NI with a view to identifying, prosecuting and punishing perpetrators of human rights violations, in particular the right to life, and providing appropriate remedies for victims;

(b) Ensure, given the passage of time, the sufficient funding to enable the effective investigation of all outstanding cases and ensure its access to all documentation and material relevant for its investigations.[74]

On 23 December 2014 the Stormont House Agreement was reached.[75] The Agreement contains plans to address the investigation of conflict related deaths. Four bodies and one specific service to deal with 'The Past' are to be established. These are:

- The Oral History Archive, which will 'provide a central place for peoples from all backgrounds (and from throughout the UK and Ireland) to share experiences and narratives related to the Troubles.'[76]

- Victims and Survivors' 'Services', which will include a Mental Trauma Service, a proposal 'for a pension for severely physically injured victims', and advocate-counsellor assistance.[77]

- The Historical Inquiries Unit, which will 'take forward investigations into outstanding Troubles-related deaths'.[78]

- The Independent Commission on Information Retrieval, which will 'enable victims and survivors to seek and privately receive information about the (Troubles-related) deaths of their next of kin'.[79]

- The Implementation and Reconciliation Group, which will 'oversee themes, archives and information recovery' and commission an academic report after 5 years analysing themes.[80]

---

74 UN Human Rights Committee, Concluding observations on the seventh periodic report of the United Kingdom of Great Britain and Northern Ireland, CCPR/C/GBR/CO/7, UN HRC, July 2015, para 11(b).

75 NI Office, 'Stormont House Agreement', 23 December 2014.

76 NI Office, 'Stormont House Agreement', 23 December 2014, para 22.

77 NI Office, 'Stormont House Agreement', 23 December 2014, para 26-29.

78 NI Office, 'Stormont House Agreement', 23 December 2014, para 30.

79 NI Office, 'Stormont House Agreement', 23 December 2014, para 41.

80 NI Office, 'Stormont House Agreement', 23 December 2014, para 51.

The UK Government has stated that specific measures of the financial package to NI will include, 'up to £150m over 5 years to help fund the bodies to deal with the past'.[81] It further states that:

[t]he paper from the party leaders estimates the potential costs of the new bodies to be higher than Government estimates. The Government recognises the burden that this work puts on the PSNI and that the costs could be higher and so will provide further funding. Therefore the Government will contribute up to £30m per year for five years to pay for the institutions to help deal with the past.[82]

Political agreement around the establishment of the institutions envisaged by the Stormont House Agreement has not been reached and no published plan is in place for the establishment of the relevant bodies.

As reported by the Committee of Ministers 'the major obstacle is the proposed national security veto on disclosure of information to the victim's families at the conclusion of an Historical Investigations Unit investigation'.[83] The then Secretary of State for NI Theresa Villiers MP in February 2016 elaborated that:

The dispute is about onward disclosure from the HIU. And it is an inescapable fact that there is information which would put lives at risk if it were put into the public domain. There are notorious examples of where people accused of being informants have been hunted down and murdered.[84]

The Commission amongst others is concerned that momentum relating to the Agreement has waned and has raised this matter with the UN Human Rights Council.

The UK has continued to fail to implement European Court of Human Rights judgments stipulating measures to achieve effective investigations into 'Troubles-related' deaths since 2001,[85] and this failure is itself resulting in new findings of violations against the UK.[86] The Committee of Ministers has expressed deep regret that the implementation of the judgements has not occurred.[87] In June 2016 the Committee of Ministers:

called upon the authorities to take all necessary measures to ensure the Historical Investigations Unit can be established and start its work without any further delay, particularly in light of the length of time that has already passed since these judgments became final and the failure of previous initiatives to achieve effective, expeditious investigations.[88]

In his keynote speech to the September 2016 British Irish Association Conference opening event at Oxford University Secretary of State for NI Rt Hon James Brokenshire MP stated:

Over recent months my department has been fully engaged on work necessary to establish the Historical Investigations Unit, the Independent Commission for Information Retrieval, the Implementation and Reconciliation Group and the Oral History Archive.

---

81 Stormont House Agreement, Financial Annex, 2014, p1. The SHA includes a further broad financial commitment to all sections covered in the SHA; 'The total value of the Government's package is additional spending power of almost £2 billion.' Stormont House Agreement, Financial Annex, 2014, para 3.

82 Stormont House, Financial Annex, 2014, p. 2.

83 Communication from the United Kingdom concerning the McKerr group of cases against the United Kingdom (Application No. 28883/95) DH-DD(2016)430 13/04/2016

84 Northern Ireland Office and The Rt Hon Theresa Villiers MP, A way forward for legacy of the past in Northern Ireland, Ulster University, Belfast, 11 February 2016.

85 See the McKerr Group of Cases, Council of Europe, Committee of Ministers, Cases No. 25, 1201st meeting – 5 June 2014, Cases against the United Kingdom https://search.coe.int/cm/pages/result_details.aspx?objectid=090000168065dbae

86 See Hemsworth v. The United Kingdom, Application No. 58559/09, 16 October 2013.

87 Committee of Ministers, 1259th meeting – 7-8 June 2016 Item H46-42 McKerr group v. the United Kingdom (Application No. 28883/95) Supervision of the execution of the Court's judgments.

88 Committee of Ministers, 1259th meeting – 7-8 June 2016 Item H46-42 McKerr group v. the United Kingdom (Application No. 28883/95) Supervision of the execution of the Court's judgments.

The work has been shaped by many meetings with political parties, academics and victims' groups, and with the Irish Government who also have important obligations in respect of the past.

I now believe the process would benefit from a more public phase. And over the coming weeks I will reflect on what form that might take.[89]

Legacy inquests and inquiries

The UN Human Rights Committee recommended that the UK, including the NI Executive:

*Ensure that the Legacy Investigation Branch [PSNI] and the Coroner's court in NI are adequately resourced and are well-positioned to effectively review outstanding legacy case*s.[90]

The Stormont House Agreement does not contain specific commitments relating to legacy inquests but states that:

Processes dealing with the past should be victim-centred. Legacy inquests will continue as a separate process to the [Historical Inquiries Unit]. Recent domestic and European judgments have demonstrated that the legacy inquest process is not providing access to a sufficiently effective investigation within an acceptable timeframe. In light of this, the Executive will take appropriate steps to improve the way the legacy inquest function is conducted to comply with ECHR Article 2 requirements.[91]

Following his appointment as President of the Coroners court the Lord Chief Justice instigated a review of the state of readiness of 53 outstanding inquests into conflict related deaths. This was conducted by Lord Justice of Appeal Reg Weir QC who expressed concerns regarding delays and resourcing of legacy inquests.[92] In February 2016 the Lord Chief Justice met with the families awaiting legacy inquests setting out plans to address outstanding legacy inquests.[93]

The Lord Chief Justice made clear that his plans for addressing legacy inquests were contingent upon necessary resources being allocated to allow for the creation of a Legacy Inquest Unit within the NI Courts Service to support Coroners Service and the full cooperation of relevant state agencies including the Police Service NI and Ministry of Defence.

Following the initiative of the Lord Chief Justice, the Department of Justice prepared a funding request seeking to draw down funds from the allocated £150 million. On the basis that this proposal had not received the approval of the NI Executive, the UK Government did not release the necessary funds.[94] In his address at the opening of the legal year, in September 2016, the Lord Chief Justice reflected on the lack of progress and that, 'the coroners' courts will not be able to satisfy their legal obligation to deliver these inquests within a reasonable timeframe in the absence of the necessary resources'.[95] A legal action has been brought to require the NI Executive to make the necessary funds available.[96]

89   Northern Ireland Office, Secretary of State's speech to 2016 British Irish Association Conference, 9 September 2016.
90   UN Human Rights Committee, Concluding observations on the seventh periodic report of the United Kingdom of Great Britain and Northern Ireland, CCPR/C/GBR/CO/7, UN HRC, July 2015, para 11 (b).
91   NI Office, 'Stormont House Agreement', 23 December 2014.
92   Communication from the United Kingdom concerning the McKerr group of cases against the United Kingdom (Application No. 28883/95) Committee of Ministers Council of Europe, McKerr Group of Cases DH-DD(2016)430, April 2016.
93   BBC News NI, 'Legacy inquests: Lord chief justice disappointed over funding bid', 4 May 2016.
94   BBC News NI, 'Lord Chief Justice legacy inquests plan put on hold', 3 May 2016.
95   Address by the Lord Chief Justice, Sir Declan Morgan, 5 September 2016.
96   BBC News NI, 'Legacy inquests: Families launch legal bid over funding', 3 November 2016

Finucane

In 2015 the UN Human Rights Committee in 2015, which subsequently recommended that the UK:

Consider launching an official inquiry into the murder of Pat Finucane.[97]

In 2015 the Finucane family unsuccessfully challenged in the High Court the decision of the then Secretary of State of NI to hold a review into the death rather than a public inquiry of the kind recommended following a review by Judge Peter Cory.[98] The Finucane family have appealed this judgment. The hearing of the appeal initially commenced in June 2016 but is adjourned at the time of writing.

On the Runs: Administrative Scheme

In its 2015 annual statement the Commission referred to the administrative scheme, established by the UK Government through which 'comfort letters' were issued to individuals living outside of the UK, who believed they might face questioning or arrest in connection with terrorist or other criminal offences relating to the conflict in NI if they returned to the UK.[99] The Government has emphasised that the letters do 'not amount to immunity, exemption or amnesty from arrest'.[100] The Commission continues to monitor the implications of the administrative scheme and the use of the Royal Prerogative of Mercy in relation to crimes committed during the conflict in NI.

Inquiries Act 2005

The UN Human Rights Committee recommended in 2015 that the UK:

Reconsider its position on the broad mandate of the executive to suppress the publication of Inquiry reports under the Inquiries Act 2005.[101]

In 2014 a House of Lords Select Committee published a report on the operation of the 2005 Act, containing 33 recommendations.[102] The Select Committee did not recommend amendments to sections 13 and 14 of the 2005 Act, which empower Government Minsters to suspend and terminate inquiries, respectively.[103] These powers have been the principal source of concern for the Commission and others.[104] Nonetheless, of the Select Committee's 33 recommendations the Government rejected 14, including all but one recommendation relating to the independence of inquiries.[105]

Amendments to the 2015 Act proposed by the House of Lords Select Committee have not been introduced in 2016.

Rule of law: non-state actors

Police Service NI statistics for the financial year 2015/16 record three security related deaths, 36 shooting incidents and 52 bombing incidents. In addition there were 14 casualties resulting from

---

97   UN Human Rights Committee, Concluding observations on the seventh periodic report of the United Kingdom of Great Britain and Northern Ireland, CCPR/C/GBR/CO/7, UN HRC, July 2015, para 8.

98   Finucane's (Geraldine) Application 2015 NIQB 57.

99   NIHRC, Submission to the UN Human Rights Committee on the United Kingdom's Seventh Periodic Report on compliance with the International Covenant on Civil and Political Rights, May 2015, paras 6.1 and 6.2.

100 NI Office, Statement by Secretary of State following the decision to hold an independent inquiry into the operation of the OTR administrative scheme, 27 February 2014.

101 UN Human Rights Committee, Concluding observations on the seventh periodic report of the United Kingdom of Great Britain and Northern Ireland, CCPR/C/GBR/CO/7, UN HRC, July 2015, para 8.

102 House of Lords Select Committee on the Inquiries Act 2005, Report of Session 2013–14, The Inquiries Act 2005: post-legislative scrutiny, March 2014.

103 House of Lords Select Committee on the Inquiries Act 2005, Report of Session 2013–14, The Inquiries Act 2005: post-legislative scrutiny, March 2014.

104 NIHRC, Submission to the UN Human Rights Committee on the United Kingdom's Seventh Periodic Report on compliance with the International Covenant on Civil and Political Rights, May 2015, paras 6.1.2 and 6.1.3.

105 Ministry of Justice, 'Government Response to the Report of the House of Lords Select Committee on the Inquiries Act 2005', June 2014.

paramilitary style shootings and there were 58 casualties as a result of paramilitary style assaults in 2015/16.[106]

In 2016 the UN CRC Committee noted that:

In Northern Ireland, children face violence, including shootings, carried out by non-State actors involved in paramilitary-style attacks, as well as recruitment by such non-State actors.[107]

The Committee recommended that the UK Government and NI Executive:

Take immediate and effective measures to protect children from violence by non-State actors involved in paramilitary-style attacks as well as from recruitment by such actors into violent activities, including through measures relating to transitional and criminal justice.[108]

In May 2016 the then Secretary of State for NI provided the House of Commons with a written summary of the main findings from the report by Lord Carlile, the Independent Reviewer of National Security Arrangements in NI, covering the period from 1 January 2015 to 31 January 2016. In his report Lord Carlile stated:

I regard 2015 as a year of success in thwarting and detecting terrorism; whilst there is no sign of reduced ambition in the minds of terrorists, the ability of these terrorists to carry out attacks has suppressed over the years by successful attrition and arrests.[109]

In July 2016 the NI Executive published an Action Plan on tackling paramilitary activity, criminality and organised crime, modelled on the four goals of; promoting lawfulness; support for transition; tackling criminality; and addressing systemic issues.[110] The Action Plan was informed by the findings of an independent three person panel.[111] The Action Plan addressed the impact of paramilitarism on children and young people and includes a number of specific actions around discouraging young men who are at risk of becoming involved, or further involved, in paramilitary activity and to address underlying activities. A cross-departmental programme to prevent vulnerable young people being drawn into paramilitary activity will be developed to sit within an Early Intervention Transformation Programme. The Early Intervention Transformation Programme Board will develop a draft programme for consideration and approval by the Executive. This programme is to be designed in conjunction with representatives from wider civic society.

The Implementation Plan agreed in relation to the Stormont House Agreement in November 2015 proposed the establishment of a four member international body to report annually on progress towards ending continuing paramilitary activity.[112] The NI (Stormont Agreement and Implementation Plan) Act 2016 received royal assent in May 2016. The Act provides for the establishment of an Independent Reporting Commission to promote progress towards ending paramilitary activity connected with NI.[113] In September 2016 the UK Government and the Government of Ireland agreed a Treaty providing for the establishment of the Independent Reporting Commission.[114]

106   PSNI, Police Recorded Security Situation Statistics: Annual Report 1st April 2015 - 31st March 2016, NISRA, 12 May 2016, see Section 1.

107   UN Committee on the Rights of the Child, Concluding Observations on the Fifth Periodic Report of the United Kingdom of Great Britain and NI, CRC/C/GBR/CO/5, UN CRC, 12 July 2016, para 47(b).

108   UN Committee on the Rights of the Child, Concluding Observations on the Fifth Periodic Report of the United Kingdom of Great Britain and NI, CRC/C/GBR/CO/5, UN CRC, 12 July 2016, para. 47(c).

109   Report by Lord Carlile of Berriew C.B.E., Q.C. on the National Security Arrangements in Northern Ireland: Written statement - HLWS705, 12 May 2016.

110   NI Executive, 'Tackling Paramilitary Activity, Criminality and Organised Crime - Executive Action Plan', 19 July 2016.

111   Lord Alderdice, John McBurney and Prof Monica McWilliams, 'The Fresh Start Panel Report on the Disbandment of Paramilitary Groups in Northern Ireland', May 2016.

112   NI Office, 'A Fresh Start: The Stormont House Agreement and Implementation Plan', 17th November 2015, para 5.1.

113   Northern Ireland (Stormont Agreement and Implementation Plan) Act 2016, section 2.

114   NI Office Press Release, 'UK-Ireland treaty brings end to paramilitarism a step closer', 13 September 2016.

The Commission recognises as a fundamental principle that human rights must operate and can only be truly effective within the framework of the rule of law.

Prison Ombudsman

The Justice Act (NI) 2016 received royal assent on 12 May 2016. The Act, inter alia, places the Prison Ombudsman for NI on a statutory footing.[115]

During the passage of the then Justice (NI) Bill the Commission provided a detailed briefing to the Committee for Justice on the requirements of effective and independent investigation into deaths in custody.[116] The Commission recommended that the Prison Ombudsman be empowered to initiate own motion investigations to ensure that the Ombudsman can address systemic issues. To ensure that issues of abuse are appropriately addressed the Commission further recommended that the Prison Ombudsman be required to inform the police of any suspected criminal offence which comes to his or her attention when conducting an investigation.[117] Amendments to the Bill were enacted reflecting the Commission's advice.

The Justice (NI) Act 2016 in addition to making provision for effective investigations into deaths in custody, empowers the Prison Ombudsman to undertake own motion investigations and requires the Ombudsman to report any criminal offence to the PSNI for investigation.[118] The Department of Justice will shortly be publishing regulations providing further detail on the powers of the Prison Ombudsman.

115   Committee for Justice, Report on the Justice No.2 Bill (NIA 57/11-16), 14 January 2016, para 118.

116   NIHRC, 'Submission to the Committee for Justice Call for Evidence on the Justice (No. 2) Bill', September 2015.

117   Committee for Justice, Report on the Justice No.2 Bill (NIA 57/11-16), 14 January 2016, para 102.

118   Justice Act (Northern Ireland) 2016. Sections A1 and A2.

Right to liberty and security of the person

ICCPR	Article 9 Article 10 Article 11
CRPD	Article 14
ECHR	Article 5
CFREU	Article 6
CRC	Article 37 (b)

Alternatives to Imprisonment

In 2013 the UN CAT[119] Committee raised concerns about the overcrowding of prisons across the UK and recommended, a strengthening of efforts and setting of:

concrete targets to reduce the high level of imprisonment and overcrowding in places of detention, in particular through the wider use of non-custodial measures as an alternative to imprisonment, in the light of the United Nations Standard Minimum Rules for Non- custodial Measures (the Tokyo Rules) (General Assembly resolution 45/110).[120]

In 2015/16 of 1,255 adult male prisoners, 647 were serving sentences of less than 6 months and of 77 adult female prisoners 56 were serving sentences of less than 6 months.[121] This represented 53 per cent of the total number of adult prisoners. The Department of Justice has acknowledged that:

[t]he actual time served by offenders on short prison sentences provides little opportunity to address offending behaviour. Community sentences, where many offenders are under probation for a prolonged period, provide more opportunities to assist the offender to overcome the difficulties that lead the offender to reoffend.[122]

In 2016 the Department of Justice published statistics on reoffending rates for those convicted of criminal offences in 2013/14 which demonstrated that 42.5 per cent of persons released from custody reoffended within one year of release. Of those who received a supervised community disposal 33.8 per cent reoffended within one year of completion.[123]

The Prison Review Team recommended in 2011 that proposals be developed: 'to ensure that effective community sentences are the preferred method of dealing with those who would otherwise get short custodial sentences'.[124] In 2014, the Prison Review Oversight Group noted that this particular recommendation had not secured political consensus and no adequate proposals were forthcoming.[125] The Oversight Group held its final meeting in 2015, the recommendation remained outstanding.[126]

119 NIHRC, Submission to the UN Human Rights Committee on the United Kingdom's Seventh Periodic Report on compliance with the International Covenant on Civil and Political Rights, May 2015, para 8.3.

120 UN Committee against Torture, Concluding observations on the fifth periodic report of the United Kingdom of Great Britain and Northern Ireland, adopted by the Committee at its fiftieth session (6-31 May 2013), CAT/C/GBR/CO/5, UN CAT, 2013, para 31.

121 Department of Justice, 'Analytical Services Group: The Northern Ireland Prison Population 2015 and 2015/16, Research and Statistical Bulletin 24/2016', September 2016, p. 24.

122 Department of Justice, 'Consultation on a Review of Community Sentences', 26 April 2011.

123 Department of Justice, 'Analytical Services Group: Adult and Youth Reoffending in Northern Ireland (2013/14 Cohort), Research and Statistical Bulletin 23/2016', September 2016, p. 11.

124 Prison Review Team, 'Review of the Northern Ireland Prison Service Conditions, management and oversight of all prisons', Recommendation 3, October 2011.

125 Prison Review Oversights Group, 'Second Annual Report', March 2014.

126 Prison Review Oversight Group, Justice Committee Summary Report, May 2015.

In 2016 the Department of Justice announced a review of sentencing to consider, 'the legislative framework for certain categories of crime, the setting of tariffs for murder, the arrangements for unduly lenient sentences and the effectiveness of the current sentencing guidelines mechanism to enhance public confidence, consistency and transparency in sentencing'.[127]

Throughout 2016 the NI Probation Board has piloted an Enhanced Combination Order in the Court Divisions of Armagh & South Down and Ards.[128] The Enhanced Combination Order, 'aims to divert offenders from short–term custodial sentences by offering judges a more intensive community order with a focus on rehabilitation, reparation, restorative practice and desistance'.

The Commission has advised the Department of Justice to consider the introduction of effective community sentences as the preferred method of dealing with those who would otherwise receive a short term custodial sentence within the context of the sentencing review.

Imprisonment for fine default

The Commission has consistently raised concerns about the numbers of people imprisoned in NI for fine default and has reported concerns to the UN on a number of occasions.[129] The Commission notes that the imprisonment of persons for fine default has historically contributed significantly to the prison population in NI.[130]

In 2013, the UN CEDAW Committee recommended that the UK, including the NI Executive continue to develop alternative sentencing and custodial strategies for women convicted of minor offences.[131] In 2013, the UN CAT Committee called for effective diversion from the criminal justice system for non-violent women offenders convicted of minor offences.[132]

In year the Justice Act (NI) 2016 received royal assent. The Act inter alia provides for a statutory framework for the collection of fines. The new framework builds on earlier work undertaken by the Department of Justice to strengthen the fine enforcement system.[133]

The Department of Justice prison population statistical bulletin records that:

The number of fine default receptions increased during 2015 to 456 receptions from 139 the year before. Although this was a large increase the numbers of fine default receptions are still much lower than the levels during 2012 (2,473). The drop in numbers during 2013 and 2014 occurred as a direct result of the Judicial Review, which led to the temporary suspension of fine defaulters being sent to prison. The Judicial Review was concluded in 2014 and resulted in the introduction of Fine Default Hearings, hence the increase in fine default receptions during 2015, but not to the levels experienced previously.[134]

---

127 Department of Justice Press Release, 'Justice Minister announces sentencing review', 9 June 2016.

128 Probation Board NI Press Release, 'New Probation Order aims to cut short term Prison sentences', 28 September 2015.

129 See, NIHRC, Response to Department of Justice Consultation on Fine Default in Northern Ireland, October 2011; NIHRC, Submissions to the UN CEDAW Committee: Parallel Report on the 7th Periodic Report of the United Kingdom of Great Britain and Northern Ireland under the Convention on the Elimination of all Forms of Discrimination against Women, June 2013, paras 32-34; Shadow Report on the Sixth Periodic Report of the United Kingdom of Great Britain and Northern Ireland, May 2008, paras 16-19; NIHRC, Submission to the United Nations Committee Against Torture, Parallel Report on the 5th Periodic Report of the United Kingdom under the Convention Against Torture and Other Cruel, Inhuman or Degrading Treatment or Punishment, 2013, para 5.3 - 5.5; NIHRC, Annual Statement, 2012, pp. 19-20; NIHRC, Annual Statement, 2013, p. 20.

130 See Prison Population statistics at http://www.dojni.gov.uk/index/ni-prison-service/nips-population-statistics-2.htm

131 UN Committee on the Elimination of Discrimination Against Women, Concluding observations on the seventh periodic report of the United Kingdom of Great Britain and Northern Ireland, CEDAW/C/GBR/CO/7, UN CEDAW, July 2013, para 55 (b), available at http://tbinternet.ohchr.org/_layouts/treatybodyexternal/Download.aspx?symbolno =CEDAW%2fC%2fGBR%2fCO%2f7&Lang=en

132 UN Committee against Torture, Concluding observations on the fifth periodic report of the United Kingdom of Great Britain and Northern Ireland, adopted by the Committee at its fiftieth session (6-31 May 2013), CAT/C/GBR/CO/5, UN CAT, 2013, para 33, available at http://tbinternet.ohchr.org/_layouts/treatybodyexternal/ Download.aspx?symbolno=CAT%2fC%2fGBR%2fCO%2f5&Lang=en

133 Department of Justice Press Release, 'Ford highlights reforms to fine enforcement system', 2 February 2012.

134 Department of Justice, 'Analytical Services Group: The Northern Ireland Prison Population 2015 and 2015/16, Research and Statistical Bulletin 24/2016', September 2016, p. 12.

The Commission continues to monitor the impact of the new fine collection framework upon the number of individuals, in particular women, being imprisoned.

Women in prison

In June 2016 there were 40 sentenced adult female, 21 unsentenced adult female and 2 young offender female prisoners within Hydebank Wood. The average sentence length for adult females was 3.93 years and 1.42 years for young offender females. The average time on remand for adult females was 59.67 days.[135] An assessment of the 2015/2016 prison population has shown that the overall female population has decreased.[136]

It is ten years since the Commission first advised that the absence of a discrete prison facility for women and gender appropriate services in NI undermines the reformative and rehabilitative aims which imprisonment should strive towards.[137] This has been supported by the UN CAT Committee and the National Preventative Mechanism, designated under the Optional Protocol to the UN CAT, who recommended that women should no longer be held at Hydebank Wood and that a separate custodial facility should be established.[138]

Throughout 2016 there has been no advance in the planned construction of a new separate custodial facility for women. In its submission to the UN CAT Committee in January 2016, the Commission advised the Committee to request an update from the UK on the construction of a separate custodial facility for women offenders in NI.[139] The Commission has met with the Minister of Justice emphasising the need to reiterate the Department's commitment to meeting its human rights obligations through expediting the construction of a separate custodial facility. The Minister of Justice has indicated in correspondence to the Commission that the new facility will not be completed until financial year 2022/23, subject to securing adequate funding, the Commission continues to recommend that the Department of Justice expedite this project.[140]

In June 2016 the Department for Justice and Department for Health consulted on a draft strategy and action plan to ensure that children, young people and adults in contact with the criminal justice system were healthier, safer and less likely to be involved in offending behaviour.[141] In addition to advising the Department of Justice to publish details of the construction of a separate custodial facility for female prisoners in NI, the Commission advised that the strategy should set out how the healthcare needs of women would be addressed.[142]

Imprisonment of children with adults

The UN CRC Article 37(c) requires that: 'every child deprived of liberty shall be separated from adults unless it is considered in the child's best interest not to do so'.[143]

---

135 NI Prison Service, 'Analysis of NIPS Prison Population from 01/04/2015 to 30/06/2016', Department of Justice, July 2016.

136 Department of Justice, 'Analytical Services Group: The Northern Ireland Prison Population 2015 and 2015/16, Research and Statistical Bulletin 24/2016, September 2016, p. 5.

137 NIHRC, 'The Hurt Inside: The imprisonment of women and girls in NI', 2005. See also: NIHRC, 'Response to Department of Justice Prison Estate Policy Consultation', December 2012, para 33.

138 National Preventative Mechanism, 'Report on announced inspection of Ash House, Hydebank Wood Women's Prison 18 – 22 February', October 2013. 20 statutory bodies make up the UK National Preventive Mechanism of specific reference to Northern Ireland the Criminal Justice Inspector NI, the Independent Monitoring Board (NI), the Regulation and Quality Improvement Authority and the Northern Ireland Policing Board Independent Custody Visiting Scheme are included in the list of bodies.

139 NIHRC, Submission to the UN Committee against Torture 57 Session on the Sixth Periodic Report of the UK of Great Britain and NI on Compliance with the UN Convention against Torture and Other Cruel, Inhuman or Degrading Treatment or Punishment, 2016.

140 NIHRC, Submission of the Northern Ireland Human Rights Commission to the Department of Justice and Department of Health Consultation on Improving Health within Criminal Justice, 2016, para. 7.4.

141 Department of Justice and Department of Health, Improving Health with Criminal Justice, March 2016.

142 NIHRC, Submission of the Northern Ireland Human Rights Commission to the Department of Justice and Department of Health consultation on improving health within criminal justice, 2016, para 7.4.

143 CRC, Article 37 (c).

Throughout 2016 the imprisonment of children alongside adults has continued to be permissible in NI. The Criminal Justice (Children) (NI) Order 1998, makes provision for a 15-17 year old offender, considered likely to injure him or herself or others to be detained in the young offenders centre at Hydebank Wood, which accommodates offenders up to 21 years of age.

Previously the Commission noted that the Department of Justice had indicated its intention to amend the 1998 Order removing the legal basis for the imprisonment of children at Hydebank Wood.[144] This commitment has not been met in 2016. In June 2016 the UN CRC Committee recommended that the State Party, including the devolved administrations:

> *Ensure that child detainees are separated from adults in all detention settings.*[145]

The Minister of Justice, Claire Sugden has indicated in correspondence to the Commission that an administrative scheme has operated effectively to prevent the imprisonment of children at Hydebank Wood throughout 2016. The Minister has further indicated her intention to include reforms to the 1998 Order within a package of legislative measures relating to youth justice.

The remand of children

The UN CRC Article 37(b) requires that:

> *No child shall be deprived of his or her liberty unlawfully or arbitrarily. The arrest, detention or imprisonment of a child shall be in conformity with the law and shall be used only as a measure of last resort and for the shortest appropriate period of time.*[146]

In June 2016 the UN CRC Committee noted that throughout the UK, including NI:

> *The number of children in custody remains high, with disproportionate representation of ethnic minority children, children in care, and children with psycho-social disabilities, and detention is not always applied as a measure of last resort.*[147]

The Committee recommended that the State Party, including the NI Executive:

> *Establish the statutory principle that detention should be used as a measure of last resort and for the shortest possible period of time and ensure that detention is not used discriminatorily against certain groups of children.*[148]

The UN CRC Committee concluding observation reflected a similar observation of the UN Human Rights Committee in 2015, which called for actions to:

> *ensure that detention on remand of child defendants is used only as a measure of last resort and for the shortest possible period of time and that suitable bail packages are available to child defendants in Northern Ireland.*[149]

In March 2016 the then Minister of Justice, David Ford announced key findings from an internal scoping study into children in the justice system.[150] One of the recommendations emerging from the

---

144 NIHRC, The 2013 Annual Statement: Human Rights in NI, Belfast 2013, p. 21.

145 UN Committee on the Rights of the Child, Concluding Observations on the Fifth Periodic Report of the United Kingdom of Great Britain and NI, CRC/C/GBR/CO/5, UN CRC, 12 July 2016.

146 CRC, Article 37 (b).

147 UN Committee on the Rights of the Child, Concluding Observations on the Fifth Periodic Report of the United Kingdom of Great Britain and NI, CRC/C/GBR/CO/5, UN CRC, 12 July 2016, para 77.

148 UN Committee on the Rights of the Child, Concluding Observations on the Fifth Periodic Report of the United Kingdom of Great Britain and NI, CRC/C/GBR/CO/5, UN CRC, 12 July 2016, para 77.

149 NIHRC, 'Submission to the UN Committee on the Rights of the Child on the United Kingdom's Fifth Periodic Report on compliance with the UN Convention on the Rights of the Child', July 2015, para 23.

150 Minister of Justice, Children in the Justice System: Scoping Study, Ministerial Statements – in the Northern Ireland Assembly at 12:00 pm on 14th March 2016. https://www.theyworkforyou.com/ni/?id=2016-03-14.3.1&s=david+ford+scoping+study#g3.8

scoping study was, 'to develop the disposals available to the judiciary and reduce the use of custody to make it truly a measure of last resort'.[151] The current Minister of Justice has indicated that she is discussing with Ministerial colleagues how the recommendations of the scoping study can be carried forward and a package of legislative reform proposals to include measures to address bail and remand is to be developed.

The Commission continues to call for reform of the legislative framework to ensure children can be held in pre-trial detention only as a measure of last resort and to ensure appropriate investment in alternative to custody arrangements for children.

Definition of terrorism

In 2015 the Commission provided an update to the UN Human Rights Committee highlighting its support for the recommendation of the Independent Reviewer of Terrorism to reform the definition of terrorism within UK law.[152] The Committee subsequently recommended that the UK Government:

Consider revising the broad definition of terrorism to require intent to coerce, compel, or intimidate a government or section of the public, and implementing the recommendations of the Independent Reviewers of Terrorism Legislation.[153]

The present definition of terrorism used in the UK is to be found in the Terrorism Act 2000, section 1. Under section 1, 'terrorism' means the use or threat of action designed to influence the government or an international governmental organisation or to intimidate the public or a section of the public, and the use or threat is made for the purpose of advancing a political, religious or ideological cause. Section 1 goes on to list a range of actions and provides that the definition includes actions committed outside of the UK.

The May 2016 Queen's speech included proposals for a Counter-Extremism and Safeguarding Bill, this Bill is to contain a 'new civil order regime to restrict extremist activity'.[154] The Independent Reviewer of Terrorism has on a number of occasions raised concerns regarding the breadth of the definition of terrorism within the Terrorism Act 2000 and has stated: 'concerns are likely to be accentuated if a still broader definition is given to extremism, and if extremist activity becomes punishable by suppressive measures'.[155] In July 2016 the Joint Committee on Human Rights published a report on counter extremism in which it stated:

the Government has not demonstrated a need for new legislation. The current counter-terrorism, public order and equality legislation form a comprehensive framework which deals appropriately with those who promote violence. There is a danger that any new legislation may prove counter-productive.[156]

151 Minister of Justice, Children in the Justice System: Scoping Study, Ministerial Statements – in the Northern Ireland Assembly at 12:00 pm on 14th March 2016. https://www.theyworkforyou.com/ni/?id=2016-03-14.3.1&s=david+ford+scoping+study#g3.8

152 NIHRC, Submission to the UN Human Rights Committee on the United Kingdom's Seventh Periodic Report on compliance with the International Covenant on Civil and Political Rights, May 2015.

153 UN Human Rights Committee, Concluding observations on the seventh periodic report of the United Kingdom of Great Britain and Northern Ireland, CCPR/C/GBR/CO/7, UN HRC, July 2015, para 14

154 Cabinet Office, 'Queen's Speech 2016', 18 May 2016. https://www.gov.uk/government/speeches/queens-speech-2016

155 David Anderson QC, 'The Terrorism Acts in 2014: Report of the Independent Reviewer on the Operation of the Terrorism Act 2000 and Part 1 of the Terrorism Act 2006', September 2015, para 4.20-4.16 and 10.14-10.18. https://terrorismlegislationreviewer.independent.gov.uk/wp-content/uploads/2015/09/Terrorism-Acts-Report-2015-Print-version.pdf

156 House of Lords House of Commons Joint Committee on Human Rights, Counter-Extremism, Second Report of Session 2016–17, HL Paper 39 HC 105, para 107. http://www.publications.parliament.uk/pa/jt201617/jtselect/jtrights/105/105.pdf?utm_source=105&utm_medium=module&utm_campaign=modulereports

🟡 Powers of arrest under the Terrorism Act 2000

Under the Terrorism Act 2000 section 41 a constable may arrest without a warrant a person whom he reasonably suspects to be a terrorist. Of the 149 persons arrested in NI under the Terrorism Act 2000 in 2015/16, 18 were subsequently charged.[157] This represents 12 per cent of those arrested. The low proportion of suspects arrested under section 41 who are subsequently charged continues to be a source of concern.[158]

In 2015 the UN Human Rights Committee recommended that the UK Government:

Undertake a review of the exercise of arrest powers under section 41 of the Terrorism Act 2000 to ensure that the principles of necessity and proportionality are strictly observed when using such powers; ensure that any detention of suspects arrested under the Terrorism Act 2000 is based on an individualized determination that it is reasonable and necessary taking into account all the circumstances rather than on the nature of the crime; and, whilst ensuring public safety, make bail available to such persons, as recommended by the Joint Committee on Human Rights and the Independent Reviewer of Terrorism.[159]

This recommendation is outstanding.

---

157   PSNI, Police Recorded Security Situation Statistics Annual Report covering the period 1st April 2014 – 31st March 2015, Published 12 May 2015.

158   PSNI, Police Recorded Security Situation Statistics Annual Report covering the period 1st April 2014 – 31st March 2015, Published 12 May 2015, See Table 3.

159   UN Human Rights Committee, Concluding observations on the seventh periodic report of the United Kingdom of Great Britain and Northern Ireland, CCPR/C/GBR/CO/7, UN HRC, July 2015, para 14 (d).

Freedom from torture, inhuman and degrading treatment

ICCPR	Article 7
CAT	
ECHR	Article 3
CFREU	Article 4
CRPD	Article 15 Article 17
CRC	Article 37 Optional Protocol to the Convention on the Rights of the Child on the Sale of Children, Child Prostitution and Child Pornography

Prison review and conditions

The Oversight Group[160] established to review implementation of the recommendations of the Prison Review Group held its final meeting in May 2015, two of the recommendations of the Review Group remained unaddressed,[161] including recommendation 13 on the introduction of:

a joint healthcare and criminal justice strategy, covering all health and social care trusts, with a joint board overseeing commissioning processes within and outside prisons, to ensure that services exist to support diversion from custody and continuity of care.[162]

Healthcare provision in prisons, in particular mental health care, has been a concern for a number of years.[163] Closely related to the issue of mental health is the issue of substance abuse, both legal and illegal.[164] The Prison Ombudsman reported in 2015 that the abuse of legal highs and prescribed medications featured in many situations in which prisoners almost lost their lives and that: '[t]he trend of prisoners abusing illicit substances appears to be increasing and is a major concern since it poses very serious risk to life'. In September 2016 the Prison Ombudsman published a report into the death of Patrick Kelly in March 2015 which identified concerns around medication management.[165]

In November 2015 a report on an independent inspection of Maghaberry Prison revealed that significant failures in local leadership combined with an ineffective relationship within senior management of the NI Prison Service, contributed to the prison becoming unsafe and unstable for prisoners and staff.[166] A follow up report by the National Preventative Mechanism in July 2016 found that the Prison had 'stabilised' but significant work is required to make the prison safer for prisoners and staff. Speaking at the launch of the report Martin Lomas, Her Majesty's Deputy Chief Inspector of Prisons in England and Wales stated:

While some aspects of primary health care had improved since May 2015, it was very worrying that mental health provision had deteriorated as a result of staff shortages and now needed urgent attention.[167]

---

160 Assembly Oral Question 8899/11-16; Separately the National preventative Mechanism has recommended the establishment of a comprehensive substance misuse strategy, 'The Safety of Prisoners held by the Northern Ireland Prison Service', CJINI and RQIA, October 2014.

161 Prison Review Oversight Group, Justice Committee Summary Report, May 2015.

162 Prison Review Team, 'Review of the Northern Ireland Prison Service Conditions, management and oversight of all prisons', October 2011, p. 44.

163 Prison Review Team, 'Review of the Northern Ireland Prison Service Conditions, management and oversight of all prisons', October 2011, pp. 40 – 47.

164 Prison Review Team, 'Review of the Northern Ireland Prison Service Conditions, management and oversight of all prisons', October 2011, pp. 40 – 47.

165 Prisoner Ombudsman, 'Investigation Report into the circumstances surrounding the death of Patrick Kelly on 20th March 2015', 29th August 2016.

166 CJINI, 'Report on an unannounced inspection of Maghaberry Prison 11–22 May 2015', November 2015.

167 National Preventative Mechanism, 'Overview of initial findings of a report on an announced inspection of Maghaberry Prison 4-15 January 2016', February 2016.

On 23 November 2016 the National Preventative Mechanism published a report on an announced visit to Maghaberry Prison. Speaking during the launch of the report Brendan McGuigan, Chief Inspector of Criminal Justice in NI stated:

Inspectors found that while mental health support and assistance provided to new prisoners has improved since January 2016, there was still no overall safer joint custody strategy in place to comprehensively address safety issues, for those who were vulnerable. This is a serious omission which was impeding work in tackling vulnerability.[168]

The Commission briefed the UN Human Rights Committee in 2015 on prison conditions and highlighted the contributory influence the misuse of substances has on the mental health of prisoners and rates of suicides in prison.[169] The UN Human Rights Committee recommended robust measures:

to prevent self inflicted deaths (suicides), including suicides and self-harm in custody, inter alia by: (a) Studying and addressing the root causes of the problem, continuing improving the identification of persons at risk of suicide and self-harm and operating effective early prevention strategies and programmes;(b) Providing adequate training to prison officials on suicide and self-harm prevention; (c) Ensuring adequate protection of, and appropriate mental health and other support services to, prisoners;(d) Combating bullying in custody facilities effectively.[170]

In 2016 the Department of Justice and Department of Health consulted on a strategy to improve health within the criminal justice system. The draft strategy considered the health needs of prisoners. The Commission responded advising on the need to address the recommendation made by the UN Human Rights Committee and to ensure the strategy addresses both the health and social care needs of prisoners.[171]

Strip searches

The Commission has previously acknowledged that the NI Prison Service is committed to the development of a modern approach to searching persons that is less intrusive than the current methods.[172] A trial of millimetre wave scanning equipment had proved unsuccessful and preparation was being made to pilot an x-ray scanner. The pilot of the x-ray scanner was also delayed due to the need to obtain statutory approvals. The Commission has been informed that an alternative approach to strip searches has not yet been identified. However it is noted that the Department of Justice continue to consider options.

On 15 March 2016 the NI High Court granted an order of certiorari quashing the policy of the NI Prison Service by which forced strip search procedures are recorded on a video camera and then retained for a period of 6 years. The High Court found that: 'a search involving the removal of clothing engages ECHR Article 8. Nakedness is inherently private and forcing it upon someone cannot but engage one's right to privacy'. As such an interference with Article 8 must be 'in accordance with law' with a sufficient basis in domestic law, the High Court considered 'the policy of video recording full searches of prisoners are manifestly insufficient to provide such a basis'.[173] The Minister of Justice has indicated that she is considering the judgement.

---

168 Criminal Justice Inspectorate.

169 NIHRC, 'Submission to the UN Human Rights Committee on the Seventh Periodic Report of the UK on compliance with the ICCPR', May 2015; See further: CJINI and RQIA, 'The Safety of Prisoners held by the Northern Ireland Prison Service', October 2014.

170 UN Human Rights Committee, Concluding observations on the seventh periodic report of the United Kingdom of Great Britain and Northern Ireland, CCPR/C/GBR/CO/7, UN HRC, July 2015, para 16.

171 NIHRC, Submission of the Northern Ireland Human Rights Commission to the Department of Justice and Department of Health consultation on improving health within criminal justice, 2016.

172 Committee for Justice, 'Prison Service Reform Programme: Update', Official Report (Hansard) Session: 2012/2013, 16 May 2013.

173 Flannigan's Application [2016] NIQB 27.

Abuse in health and social care settings

The Mental Capacity (NI) Act 2016 received royal assent on 9 May 2016. The Act, inter alia, makes provision for a statutory definition of restraint and proposes a new offence of ill treatment or wilful neglect where a person lacks capacity.[174]

During the passage of the Bill, the Commission advised that the Bill should provide a free standing offence for an individual, who has the care of another individual by virtue of being a care worker, to ill-treat or wilfully neglect that individual.[175] This would reflect provisions within the Criminal Justice and Courts Act 2015 which applies to England and Wales. The Bill was not amended to provide for a free standing offence.

The Commission continues to highlight the need to ensure the criminal law framework is sufficiently robust to protect individuals reliant upon others for their health and social care needs.

Historical abuse of children and adults

On 8 July 2016, the Historical Institutional Abuse Inquiry concluded the programme of hearings which began in January 2014. Legal proceedings, which sought to have the inquiry into abuse in Kincora Boys Home heard in England at the Independent Inquiry into Child Sexual Abuse, were dismissed in April 2016.[176] The evidence into the former State run home was subsequently heard by the Historical Institutional Abuse Inquiry. The Inquiry report is now expected in January 2017 and shall be published no later than 18 January 2017.[177] The report will consider, inter alia, the: 'requirement or desirability for redress to be provided by the institution and/or the Executive to meet the particular needs of victims'.[178]

In November 2015 the Chairman of the Inquiry announced that:

> *... from the evidence we have heard so far we will recommend that there should be a scheme to award financial compensation to those children who suffered abuse in children's homes and other institutions in Northern Ireland between 1922 and 1995.*[179]

Victims of abuse who have provided evidence to the inquiry have suffered with the consequences of abuse for many years and a number are of advanced age.[180] A number of groups representing the victims of institutional abuse have raised concerns regarding the delay in setting up a redress scheme for survivors. Representatives from the Panel of Experts on Redress appeared before the Committee for the Executive Office on 28 September 2016 to press for a scheme to be set up as soon as possible.[181] After the meeting, the Executive Office stated it would be inappropriate to pre-empt the findings of the Inquiry and that 'the nature or level of any potential redress, as stipulated in the inquiry's terms of reference, is a matter the Executive will discuss and agree following receipt of the inquiry's report'.[182]

174   NIHRC, 'Submission to the Ad Hoc Committee on the Mental Capacity (NI) Bill', 2015.

175   Criminal Justice and Courts Act 2015, c. 2.

176   BBC News NI, 'Kincora Boys Home to remain part of Historical Institutional Abuse inquiry', 8 April 2016.

177   Inquiry into Historical Institutional Abuse (Amendment of Terms of Reference) Order (Northern Ireland) 2015.

178   Historical Institutional Abuse Inquiry - Terms of Reference.

179   BBC News NI, 'HIA: Chairman announces a further six institutions to be investigated', 4 November 2015.

180   NI Assembly debate Inquiry into Historical Institutional Abuse (Amendment of Terms of Reference) Order (Northern Ireland) 2015, Executive Committee Business – in the Northern Ireland Assembly, 11:15 am 3rd February 2015.

181   The Irish News, 'Government has shied away from compensation for historical abuse victims, campaigners say', 28 September 2016.

182   BBC News NI, 'Abuse survivors felt 'belittled' during meeting with head of Catholic Church in Ireland' 28 September 2016

The Commission has continued to advise the UK Government and NI Executive of the need to ensure thorough and effective investigations into all allegations of abuse.[183] The Commission notes that the Inquiry's remit did not extend to adult residents of Magdalene laundry type institutions or those abused in private settings. It has highlighted that the NI Executive should set out how the victims of such human rights violations and abuses, outside the remit of the current Inquiry, can access thorough and effective independent investigations.[184] Furthermore, the Commission has advised that such processes must be open to public scrutiny and ensure the involvement of victims. They must be capable of leading to the identification and punishment of perpetrators, of establishing the truth, and of providing an effective remedy.

Domestic violence

Statistics

Statistics collated by the Police Service of NI record that domestic violence has increased year on year since 2004/05, with the exception of two decreases recorded, a 1.6 percent decrease between 2006/07 - 2007/08 and a 7.3 per cent decrease between 2009/10 - 2010/11. The figure of 28,465 incidents for July 2015 to June 2016 is the highest level recorded since 2004/05, and shows an increase of 0.3 per cent on the 2014/15. Of the 28,465 incidents recorded in the twelve months to 30 June 2016, 12,657 incidents contained one or more crimes (amounting to 14,220 recorded crimes in total).[185]

The UN ICESCR Committee highlighted in its 2016 concluding observations on the UK that the significant rise in homelessness in NI affected victims of domestic violence amongst other vulnerable groups. The UN ICESCR Committee urged the UK:

to take immediate measures, including allocating appropriate funds to local authorities... to ensure adequate provision of reception facilities, including emergency shelters, hostels and reception, as well as social rehabilitation centres.[186]

Domestic Violence Strategy

In December 2013 the Department of Justice and the Department of Health, Social Services and Public Safety (now the Department of Health) issued a public consultation on the strategy 'Stopping Domestic and Sexual Violence and Abuse in NI, 2013-2020'. The Commission responded to the consultation advising that the binding nature of relevant international human rights standards was not recognised in the draft strategy.[187] The Commission advised that the Departments should consider the role of the strategy in ensuring that the NI Executive fulfils its obligations. The Special Rapporteur on Violence against Women following her 2014 mission to the UK recommended that:

the UK Government and devolved administrations implement comprehensive and co-ordinated strategies to prevent and combat violence against women and girls, introduce robust monitoring and accountability mechanisms to monitor the impact of these strategies, and ensure the provision of services for victims.[188]

---

183 NIHRC Correspondence from Interim Chair John Corey to Home Secretary Rt. Hon. Theresa May MP June 2014.

184 NIHRC, 'Submission to the UN Human Rights Committee on the Seventh Periodic Report of the UK on compliance with the ICCPR', May 2015, para 6.17-6.19.

185 PSNI, Domestic Abuse Incidents and Crimes Recorded by the Police in NI: Quarterly Update to 30 June 2016, August 2016.

186 UN Committee on Economic, Social and Cultural Rights, Concluding observations on the sixth periodic report of the United Kingdom of Great Britain and Northern Ireland E/C.12/GBR/CO/6, UN Economic and Social Council, 14 July 2016, paras 51 and 52.

187 NIHRC, 'Response to the Public Consultation on the Draft Strategy on Stopping Domestic and Sexual Violence and Abuse in NI, 2013-2020', May 2014.

188 UK National Human Rights Institutions Oral statement on the Special Rapporteur on violence against women country report on the United Kingdom and Northern Ireland, Human Rights Council, 29th Session, Item 3, 16 June 2015.

The former Department of Health, Social Services and Public Safety (now Department of Health) and Department of Justice published the 'Stopping Domestic and Sexual Violence and Abuse in NI Strategy' in March 2016.[189] The seven-year strategy aims to stop domestic and sexual violence and abuse in NI. It includes reference to international human rights obligations and standards.

The Commission recommended to the UN ICESCR Committee in 2016 that the UK provide an update on the implementation of the Stopping Domestic Violence and Sexual Abuse Strategy in NI.[190]

Domestic Violence Offences

In early 2016 the Department of Justice consulted on whether there should be a specific offence that captured patterns of coercive and controlling behaviour.[191] It also consulted on the establishment of a Domestic Violence Disclosure Scheme in NI, based on processes which would enable new partners to obtain details of a partner's previous history of violence and abuse. In October 2016 the Minister of Justice indicated her intention to bring forward legislation to criminalise coercive and controlling behaviour as a matter of priority.[192]

The Commission recommended to the UN ICESCR Committee in 2016 that the UK took note of the consultation on offences that captured coercive behaviour and domestic violence disclosure scheme and recommended similar provision in NI as exists in other parts of the UK.[193]

UN Security Council Resolution 1325

Reporting on her 2014 mission to the UK, the Special Rapporteur on Violence against Women noted concerns in NI: 'regarding the exclusion of women from the peace-building processes and how their experiences of violence during and after the conflict have been mostly unrecognized'.[194] The Special Rapporteur recommended that the UK ensure the full implementation in NI of UN Security Council resolution 1325.[195] The Commission, along with the other UK national human rights institutions, made an oral intervention at the UN Human Rights Council in 2015 welcoming the publication of the Special Rapporteur's Report.

Istanbul Convention

The UK Government has signed the Council of Europe Convention on preventing and combating violence against women and domestic violence (the Istanbul Convention) and the Home Office is working with the devolved administrations and other government departments to develop a time-frame for ratification. A Private Members' Bill, 'Preventing and Combating Violence against Women and Domestic Violence (Ratification of Convention)', brought by Dr Elidih Whiteford calling for the UK to ratify the Istanbul Convention was also submitted to the UK Parliament in 2016. It passed its first reading and will be considered at its second reading in December 2016.[196]

189 Department of Health, Social Services and Public Safety and Department of Justice, Stopping Domestic and Sexual Violence and Abuse in Northern Ireland: A Seven Year Strategy, March 2016.

190 NIHRC, Submission to the UN Committee on Economic, Social and Cultural Rights 58th Session on the Sixth Periodic Report of the United Kingdom's Compliance with ICESCR, April 2016, p. 40.

191 Department of Justice, Domestic Abuse Offence and Domestic Violence Disclosure Scheme, 2016.

192 Domestic Abuse, Rape and Sexual Crime Private Members' Business – in the Northern Ireland Assembly at 4:15 pm on 17th October 2016.

193 NIHRC, Submission to the UN Committee on Economic, Social and Cultural Rights 58th Session on the Sixth Periodic Report of the United Kingdom's Compliance with ICESCR, April 2016, p. 40.

194 Report of the Special Rapporteur on violence against women, its causes and consequences, Rashida Manjoo Addendum, Mission to the United Kingdom of Great Britain and Northern Ireland, 19 May 2015.

195 Report of the Special Rapporteur on violence against women, its causes and consequences, Rashida Manjoo Addendum, Mission to the United Kingdom of Great Britain and Northern Ireland, 19 May 2015, para 106 (c) (x).

196 http://services.parliament.uk/bills/2016-17/preventingandcombatingviolenceagainstwomenanddomesticviolenceratificationofconvention.html

The Commission advised that the Department of Justice and the Department of Health, Social Services and Public Safety (now the Department of Health) should take cognisance of the Istanbul Convention in the Domestic Violence Strategy for NI.[197] The 'Stopping Domestic and Sexual Violence and Abuse in NI Strategy' refers to the Istanbul Convention.[198]

Non-nationals and Domestic Violence

The no recourse to public funds rule prevents persons with insecure immigration status from accessing benefits, such as refuge support. The Destitute Domestic Violence concession was introduced by the then UK Border Agency on 1 April 2012. This concession aims to help non-nationals who are victims of domestic violence and on a spousal visa to leave their partner safely and secure their immigration in the UK. The concession offers those who meet the eligibility criteria temporary leave for three months, enabling them to apply for access to public funds. During this three month period the person should make a separate application for indefinite leave to remain under the Domestic Violence rule.[199] There are strict eligibility criteria for the concession and so there are some groups who may not benefit. The Commission recommended in its 2016 submission to the UN ICESCR Committee that the UK extend provision for victims of domestic violence to persons who enter the UK other than on a spousal visa.[200]

🟠 Allegations of torture and cruel, inhuman or degrading treatment or punishment overseas

In its 2014 annual statement the Commission recorded that the UK Government has accepted the credibility of a number of allegations of complicity of British military personnel, security and secret intelligence services in the ill-treatment of detainees overseas. The Commission's view is that investigations by the UK Government into these allegations have not satisfied the investigative duty under Articles 2 and 3 of the ECHR, nor its obligations under the UN CAT.[201]

In June 2015 the Commission, in conjunction with the other UK NHRIs, addressed the UN Human Rights Council highlighting:

that the delay reinforces the need for a full, independent, judge-led inquiry which complies with the investigative obligation under international human rights law.[202]

In its concluding observations on the ICCPR the UN Human Rights Committee called on the UK to:

Address the excessive delays in the investigation of cases dealt with by the Iraq Historical Allegations Team and consider establishing more robust accountability measures to ensure prompt, independent, impartial and effective investigations.[203]

---

197 NIHRC, Response to the Public Consultation on the Draft Strategy on Stopping Domestic and Sexual Violence and Abuse in Northern Ireland, 2013-2020, May 2014, para 2.10.

198 Department of Health, Social Services and Public Safety and Department of Justice, Stopping Domestic and Sexual Violence and Abuse in Northern Ireland: A Seven Year Strategy, March 2016, para 2.18.

199 NRPF Network, The Destitution Domestic Violence (DDV) Concession, 2013.

200 NIHRC, Submission to the UN Committee on Economic, Social and Cultural Rights 58th Session on the Sixth Periodic Report of the United Kingdom's Compliance with ICESCR, 2016, pp. 38-40.

201 See NIHRC, EHRC and SHRC, 'Follow-up regarding Concluding Observations adopted by the Committee Against Torture on the 5th periodic report of the UK', September 2014, p. 3.

202 Joint Oral Statement submitted by the NIHRC, EHRC, and the SHRC, 'Report of the Special Rapporteur on the promotion and protection of human rights and fundamental freedoms while countering terrorism', UN Human Rights Council 29th Session, Agenda Item 3, June 2015.

203 UN Human Rights Committee, Concluding observations on the seventh periodic report of the United Kingdom of Great Britain and Northern Ireland, CCPR/C/GBR/CO/7, UN HRC, July 2015, para 9 (b).

In October 2015 the newly appointed chair of the Intelligence and Security Committee made a statement to the House of Commons on its forward work plan.[204] The plan identified a number of immediate priorities and stated:

> *Our longer-term priority is the substantial Inquiry into the role of the UK Government and Security and Intelligence Agencies in relation to detainee treatment and rendition, where there are still unanswered questions.*[205]

In July 2016 the Intelligence and Security Committee published an annual report for the financial year 2015/16 in which it recorded:

> *The Committee has taken evidence from the three intelligence and security Agencies, the Foreign Secretary and the Home Secretary. Further evidence sessions are planned with those individuals who were involved at the time, including former Ministers and Agency staff. It is a detailed and long-term Inquiry into an important issue and is expected to occupy the Committee for some time.*[206]

In October 2016 the Minister of Defence the Rt. Hon Michael Fallon MP issued a statement declaring the Government's:

> *intention to derogate from the ECHR, if possible in the circumstances that exist at that time, will protect British troops serving in future conflicts from the kind of persistent legal claims that have followed recent operations in Iraq and Afghanistan on an industrial scale.*[207]

Deprivation of citizenship

In 2014 the Westminster Parliament amended the British Nationality Act 1981, empowering the Home Secretary to deprive a naturalised British citizen of their citizenship if they have engaged in conduct 'seriously prejudicial' to the UK's vital interests, and the Home Secretary has reasonable grounds to believe the person is able, under the law of a country or territory outside the UK, to become a national of such a country or territory. The UK Government may exercise powers to deprive an individual of their citizenship both when they are in the UK and when they are abroad.[208]

In April 2016 the Independent Reviewer of Terrorism published a report into the operation of the power in the first 12 months.[209] The Independent Reviewer noted:

> *The power under review was not exercised during the period under review, and indeed had still not been exercised as of April 2016, when this report went to print. There is therefore no concrete action to review.*[210]

204 The Rt. Hon. Dominic Grieve QC, MP, Chairman of the Intelligence and Security Committee of Parliament, 'Intelligence and Security Committee – Work Priorities Statement', October 2015.

205 Intelligence and Security Committee – Work Priorities Statement The Rt. Hon. Dominic Grieve QC, MP, Chairman of the Intelligence and Security Committee of Parliament.

206 Intelligence and Security Committee of Parliament, 'Annual Report 2015–2016', 5 July 2016

207 Ministry of Defence: Press Release, 'Government to protect armed forces from persistent legal claims in future overseas operations', 4 October 2016.

208 Melanie Gower, 'Deprivation of British Citizenship and withdrawal of passport facilities' SN/HA/6820, House of Commons Library, 30 January 2015.

209 David Anderson Q.C. Independent Reviewer of Terrorism Legislation, Citizenship Removal resulting in statelessness: First Report of the Independent Reviewer on the Operation of the Power to Remove Citizenship Obtained by Naturalisation from Persons who have other Citizenship, April 2016.

210 David Anderson Q.C. Independent Reviewer of Terrorism Legislation, Citizenship Removal resulting in statelessness: First Report of the Independent Reviewer on the Operation of the Power to Remove Citizenship Obtained by Naturalisation from Persons who have other Citizenship, April 2016, para 1.9.

The Independent Reviewer further noted the breadth of the discretion afforded to the Home Secretary and the absence of a requirement to obtain judicial consent before exercise of the power.[211] He stated:

The power under review is an unusually strong one in international terms. It extends further than the laws of most comparable countries in Europe, North America or Australasia… It remains to be seen whether the power will be used in future – or, if used, whether it will be of any practical benefit in the global fight against terrorism. [212]

The UN Human Rights Committee has recommended:

The State party should review its laws to ensure that restrictions on re-entry and denial of citizenship on terrorism grounds include appropriate procedural protections, and are consistent with the principles of legality, necessity and proportionality. The State party should also ensure that appropriate standards and procedures are in place to avoid rendering an individual stateless.[213]

The Counter Terrorism and Security Act 2015 provides for Temporary Exclusion Orders. These prohibit the return of an individual to the UK unless the return is in accordance with a permit to return.[214] The Act makes provision for an individual subject to a Temporary Exclusion Order to be able to apply to the court for a statutory review of the Order on their return to the UK.[215] The UK Government has stated that, 'It is not possible to predict how many temporary exclusion orders will be served'.[216] During the passage of the Act the Commission provided a briefing to a number of NI peers emphasising the need for appropriate judicial safeguards.[217] A report on the use of Temporary Exclusion Orders is awaited.[218]

Mechanisms to identify victims of torture detained in immigration facilities

In NI irregular migrants are detained at Larne House short term holding facility.[219] Detainees are held for a maximum period of five or seven days, if Removal Directions are in place. Detainees are then released, transferred to Immigration Removal Centres elsewhere in the UK or removed, including to Ireland.

The Immigration Detention Centre Rules make provision for the regulation and management of detention centres.[220] The Rules provide for matters such as the welfare and health care of immigration detainees. Rule 35 (3) of the Detention Centre Rules places an obligation on a medical practitioner to report to the manager of the Centre any detained person who he/she is concerned may have been the victim of torture. In 2013 the UN CAT Committee had recommended that the UK Government:

conduct an immediate independent review of the application of Rule 35 of the Detention Centre Rules in immigration detention, in line with the Home Affairs Committee's recommendation and ensure that similar rules apply to short term holding facilities.[221]

---

211   David Anderson Q.C. Independent Reviewer of Terrorism Legislation, Citizenship Removal resulting in statelessness: First Report of the Independent Reviewer on the Operation of the Power to Remove Citizenship Obtained by Naturalisation from Persons who have other Citizenship, April 2016, para 3.16.

212   David Anderson Q.C. Independent Reviewer of Terrorism Legislation, Citizenship Removal resulting in statelessness: First Report of the Independent Reviewer on the Operation of the Power to Remove Citizenship Obtained by Naturalisation from Persons who have other Citizenship, April 2016, para 4.9.

213   UN Human Rights Committee, Concluding observations on the seventh periodic report of the United Kingdom of Great Britain and Northern Ireland, CCPR/C/GBR/CO/7, UN HRC, July 2015, para 15.

214   Counter-Terrorism and Security Act 2015, Section 2 (1)(a).

215   Counter Terrorism and Security Act 2015, Section 10.

216   Counter-Terrorism and Security Act 2015 - Temporary Exclusion Orders – Royal Assent IA No: HO0144 11, February 2014.

217   Correspondence dispatched from the Chief Commissioner to NI Members of the House of Lords, January 2015.

218   cW Diana R. Johnson Shadow Minister (Foreign and Commonwealth Affairs), Hansard HC Deb, 5 January 2016.

219   The UKBA has informed the Commission that at Larne House "The Detention Centre Rules do not apply." Email correspondence between UKBA and NIHRC dated 26 March 2013.

220   Immigration Detention Centre Rules 2001.

221   UN Committee against Torture, Concluding observations on the fifth periodic report of the United Kingdom of Great Britain and Northern Ireland, adopted by the Committee at its fiftieth session (6-31 May 2013), CAT/C/GBR/CO/5, UN CAT, 2013, para 30.

The Detention Centre Rules do not apply to Larne House due to its classification as a short term holding facility. Measures in place for the identification of victims of torture in Larne House appear to rely heavily on self identification.

In January 2016 Stephen Shaw, the former Prisoner and Probation Ombudsman for England & Wales published a report into his review of the welfare of immigration detainees, which was commissioned by the Home Office.[222] In his report, Stephen Shaw noted the absence of rules governing short term holding centres and recommended that a discussion draft of the short term holding centre rules be published as a matter of urgency. In addition Stephen Shaw recommended:

> *that the Home Office immediately consider an alternative to the current rule 35 mechanism. This should include whether doctors independent of the IRC system (for example, Forensic Medical Examiners) would be more appropriate to conduct the assessments as well as the training implications.*[223]

In responding to the report Lord Bates, the Parliamentary Under-Secretary of State, Home Office stated that the Government will 'strengthen our processes for dealing with those cases of torture'.[224] However substantive proposals around the application of Rule 35 or the rules governing short term holding centres have not yet been agreed.

Female genital mutilation

There are no systematic estimates of the prevalence of female genital mutilation in NI. Nevertheless, there is anecdotal evidence from the Royal College of Nursing and non-governmental organisations that female genital mutilation is present in NI.[225]

In 2014 the Commission welcomed the former Department of Finance and Personnel's (now Department of Finance) targeted consultation on draft 'Multi-Agency Practice Guidelines on Female Genital Mutilation'.[226] The Guidelines provide advice and support to frontline professionals who are responsible for safeguarding children and protecting adults from the abuses associated with female genital mutilation.

The Commission advised the Department of Finance and Personnel (now the Department of Finance) that human rights law requires the NI Executive to modify social and cultural patterns which see women as subordinate to men. Female genital mutilation is a severe form of child abuse and a violation of human rights, as well as a manifestation of deeply entrenched gender inequality and patriarchal cultural norms.

The NI Executive approved the publication of the Multi-Agency Practice Guidelines in July 2014. The Commission welcomed the robust measures initiated to combat this ongoing human rights abuse. The Commission considers that the Practice Guidelines and initiatives by the NI Executive should be supported by an action plan to ensure the Guidelines are operationalised. The Commission has written to the relevant NI Executive Ministers to seek assurance that a detailed action plan is developed to include; training; awareness raising; research into the prevalence of female genital mutilation; implementation of regional guidance; care pathways; and actions which can be taken to identify and prosecute perpetrators.

---

222 A Report to the Home Office by Stephen Shaw, Review into the Welfare in Detention of Vulnerable Persons, Cm 9186, January 2016.

223 A Report to the Home Office by Stephen Shaw, Review into the Welfare in Detention of Vulnerable Persons, Cm 9186, January 2016, Recommendation 21.

224 Lord Bates (The Parliamentary Under-Secretary of State, Home Office), 'Immigration Detention: Response to Stephen Shaw's report into the Welfare in Detention of Vulnerable Persons:Written statement' - HLWS462, 14 January 2016.

225 NIHRC, Female Genital Mutilation in the United Kingdom, August 2016, p.10.

226 Multi-Agency Practice Guidelines: Female Genital Mutilation, January 2014.

In January 2016 the Safeguarding Board NI agreed that female genital mutilation would be added to the Learning Development Strategy framework.[227] A Safeguarding Board NI led practice network to prevent Female Genital Mutilation has also been set up.[228] An action plan for the network is yet to be published.

In August 2016, the Commission published a report on female genital mutilation in the UK.[229] This report clarified the obligations that the UK has under international and regional human rights law regarding the effective eradication of female genital mutilation within the UK. It was submitted to the Home Affairs Committee's 'Female Genital Mutilation Follow-up Inquiry'. The Inquiry's report, published in September 2016, called for greater awareness of female genital mutilation and stressed the duty on frontline professionals to report incidences of female genital mutilation.[230]

Syrian refugee crisis

In September 2015 in response to the refugee crisis the UK Government committed to receive 20,000 Syrian refugees.[231] This commitment has been criticised for not representing a: 'fair and proportionate share of refugees, both those already within the EU and those still outside it'.[232]

On 27 July 2016 the Minister of State for the Home Office informed the House of Commons:

We continue to work with local authorities and International Partners to deliver the Government's commitment to resettle 20,000 Syrian refugees by the end of this Parliament. We are on track to do this. The number resettled in a particular period will depend on a range of factors including the flow of referrals from the United Nations High Commissioner for Refugees and the availability of suitable accommodation and support in the UK. Progress on resettlement is indicated in quarterly immigration statistics.[233]

In September 2016 the Minister for Communities, Paul Givan informed the NI Assembly that:

To date, four groups of Syrian refugees, comprising 221 people in total, have come to Northern Ireland under the UK Government's Syrian Vulnerable Persons Relocation Scheme. Two more groups totalling an estimated 160 people are expected to arrive before the end of 2016. I can advise that the plans which were put in place by Department to manage the arrival and settlement of the refugees are working very effectively and the quality of the support systems is helping them to integrate into Northern Ireland society. An ability to speak and understand English will be crucial to the success of the refugees' integration and I am pleased to report that all of the refugees who have arrived so far are accessing English language lessons and are making very good progress in developing their English skills.[234]

In 2016, the Commission raised concerns about the outstanding Refugee Integration Strategy to the UN CERD Committee.[235] The European Commission against Racism and Intolerance has also recommended that a refugee integration strategy is developed in NI 'to assist newly-arrived refugees,

---

227 Safeguarding Board for Northern Ireland, Minutes of the 20th Meeting of the Safeguarding Board for Northern Ireland, 14 January 2016.

228 The Irish News, 'FGM now an emerging issue in Northern Ireland', 3 August 2016. http://www.irishnews.com/opinion/letterstotheeditor/2016/08/03/news/some-are-in-no-position-to-point-sectarian-finger-at-others-633567/

229 NIHRC, Female Genital Mutilation in the United Kingdom, August 2016.

230 House of Commons Home Affairs Committee, Female Genital Mutilation: Abuse Unchecked, Ninth Report of Session 2016-17, HC 390, House of Commons, 15 September 2016.

231 BBC News, 'UK to accept 20,000 refugees from Syria by 2020', 7 September 2015.

232 Lawyers Refugee Initiative, 'Refugee Crisis, Call from the Legal Community for Urgent Action', 12th October 2015.

233 Refugees: Syria:Written question - HL1202, Asked by Lord Roberts of Llandudno, 13 July 2016.

234 AQW 4216/16-21 28/09/2016.

235 NIHRC, Submission to the United Nations Committee on the Elimination of Racial Discrimination: Parallel Report on the 21st to 23rd Periodic Reports of the United Kingdom under the International Convention on the Elimination of All forms of Racial Discrimination, July 2016, para 65.

in particular as concerns housing, employment, access to welfare and learning English, and that refugee integration is systematically evaluated'.[236]

Corporal punishment of children

The Law Reform (Miscellaneous Provisions) (NI) Order 2006 continues to allow for a defence of reasonable chastisement of a child, and provides that this is a defence to a charge of common assault tried summarily. In Ireland, the Children Act 2011 and Children First Act 2015 abolished the statutory and common law defence of reasonable chastisement respectively.

In July 2016 the UN CRC Committee again recommended an abolition of corporal punishment of children in the UK, recommending that the UK Government and devolved administrations:

(a) Prohibit as a matter of priority all corporal punishment in the family, including through the repeal of all legal defences, such as "reasonable chastisement";

(b) Ensure that corporal punishment is explicitly prohibited in all schools and educational institutions and all other institutions and forms of alternative care;

(c) Strengthen its efforts to promote positive and non-violent forms of discipline and respect for children's equal right to human dignity and physical integrity, with a view to eliminating the general acceptance of the use of corporal punishment in child-rearing.[237]

---

236 European Commission against Racism and Intolerance, Report on the United Kingdom (fifth monitoring cycle), CRI(2016)38, Adopted on 29 June 2016, European Commission against Racism and Intolerance, 4 October 2016, para 116.

237 UN Committee on the Rights of the Child, Concluding Observations on the Fifth Periodic Report of the United Kingdom of Great Britain and NI, CRC/C/GBR/CO/5, UN CRC, 12 July 2016, para 40.

Freedom from slavery

ICCPR	Article 8
ECHR	Article 4
CFREU	Article 5
CRC	Article 34 Optional Protocol to the Convention on the Rights of the Child on the sale of children, child prostitution and child pornography

Child sexual exploitation

An Independent Inquiry into Child Sexual Exploitation in NI was initiated by the Ministers for Health, Justice and Education in 2013 and published its report in November 2014. The Inquiry report includes 17 key recommendations and 60 supporting recommendations for improvement in combating child sexual exploitation, outlining measures for improved inter-agency working, education and awareness raising, training for professionals, funding of preventative services, engagement with communities, support for victims and the development of a regional strategy.[238]

The recommendations also cover the need for legislative reform in a number of areas, including addressing a gap in protection under the Sexual Offences (NI) Order 2008.[239] Presently for a number of serious sexual offences against children aged between 13 and 18 years, 'the defendant may claim that he/she believed the victim to be above 18 years' thus requiring the prosecution to prove that the defendant did not reasonably believe this.

In its 2014 report on the compatibility of the UK with the Optional Protocol on the sale of children, child prostitution and child pornography the UN CRC Committee raised concerns that:

> the Sexual Offences (NI) Order 2008, for certain grave offences of sexual exploitation of children between 13 and 16 years of age, such as meeting a child following sexual grooming, engaging in sexual activity with a child, arranging or facilitating a child sex offence, the defendant may claim that he/she believed the victim to be above 16 years.[240]

The UN CRC Committee recommended reform to the 2008 Order to include 'a provision that for child victims, the burden of proof would be reversed'.[241] The Department of Justice 'Tackling Child Sexual Exploitation in NI Action Plan' contains a commitment to consider the 2008 Order and its compatibility with international standards.[242] In September 2016 a progress report on implementation of the Action Plan was issued which recorded that: 'Work is continuing towards establishing possible provisions to bring forward for future consultation and presentation to the NI Assembly'.[243] The progress report therefore did not indicate clear progress towards implementation of the UN CRC Committee's recommendation. The Minister of Justice has informed the Commission that it is intended that proposals for reform will be subject to public consultation in April 2017.

---

238 Kathleen Marshall, 'Child Sexual Exploitation in Northern Ireland Report of the Independent Inquiry', November 2014, p. 149.

239 Kathleen Marshall, 'Child Sexual Exploitation in Northern Ireland Report of the Independent Inquiry', November 2014, Recommendation 14.

240 UN Committee on the Rights of the Child, Concluding observations on the report submitted by the United Kingdom of Great Britain and Northern Ireland under article 12, paragraph 1, of the Optional Protocol to the Convention on the Rights of the Child on the sale of children, child prostitution and child pornography, CRC/C/OPSC/GBR/CO/1, UN CRC, July 2014, para 27.

241 UN Committee on the Rights of the Child, Concluding observations on the report submitted by the United Kingdom of Great Britain and Northern Ireland under article 12, paragraph 1, of the Optional Protocol to the Convention on the Rights of the Child on the sale of children, child prostitution and child pornography, CRC/C/OPSC/GBR/CO/1, UN CRC, July 2014, para 29.

242 Department of Justice, Tackling Child Sexual Exploitation in Northern Ireland: Action Plan, March 2015 (Revised – August 2015).

243 Department of Justice, Department of Education and Department of Health, Tackling Child Sexual Exploitation in Northern Ireland: First Composite CSE Implementation Plan Progress Report 1st April 2015 to 30th September 2015, August 2016, p. 14

The Commission reported to the UN CRC Committee on the issue of child sexual exploitation once again in 2016 advising that, 'no measures have been taken to ensure that all children up to 18 years of age are protected from all types of offences covered by the Optional Protocol'.[244] In its report the UN CRC Committee noted that:

> the Sexual Offences Act (2003) in England and Wales and the Sexual Offences (NI) Order (2008) have not been revised to provide full and equal protection to all children under 18 years of age.[245]

The UN CRC Committee recommended:

> that the State party fully implement the Committee's recommendations on the initial report of the State party... provided in its concluding observations on the Optional Protocol on the sale of children, child prostitution and child pornography in particular that the State party: (a) Ensure that all children up to 18 years of age are protected from all types of offence covered by the Optional Protocol.[246]

Child, early and forced marriage

Throughout 2016 the Commission has chaired the Commonwealth Forum of National Human Rights Institutions. The Forum is an informal and inclusive body of Commonwealth National Institutions for the Promotion and Protection of Human Rights and other national accountability mechanisms with a human rights mandate. As a member of the Forum the Commission has assigned to the Kigali Declaration on the elimination of child, early and forced marriage in the Commonwealth. The Declaration notes that National Human Rights Institutions are:

> Concerned by estimates that over the next decade 140 million girls under the age of 18 years will be forced to marry and that half of these girls live in Commonwealth member states.[247]

The UN Committee on the Rights of the Child, General Comment No. 4 strongly recommends the review and, where necessary, reform of legislation and practice to increase the minimum age for marriage with and without parental consent to 18 years, for both girls and boys. [248]

The Marriage (NI) Order 2003, which is a responsibility of the Department of Finance, permits the marriage of a child aged 16 or 17 years with the consent of their parents or legal guardians or the courts. In NI, 68 children were married in 2015 of these 49 were girls and 19 were boys.[249] In May 2016 the UN CRC Committee recommended that:

> the [UK] raise the minimum age of marriage to 18 years. [250]

244 NIHRC, Submission to the UN Committee on the Rights of the Child 72nd Session on the Fifth Periodic Report of the United Kingdom of Great Britain and Northern Ireland on compliance with the UN Convention on the Rights of the Child, 15 April 2016, paras 29-31

245 UN Committee on the Rights of the Child, Concluding Observations on the Fifth Periodic Report of the United Kingdom of Great Britain and NI, CRC/C/GBR/CO/5, UN CRC, 12 July 2016, para 81(d)

246 UN Committee on the Rights of the Child, Concluding Observations on the Fifth Periodic Report of the United Kingdom of Great Britain and NI, CRC/C/GBR/CO/5, UN CRC, 12 July 2016, para 82(a)

247 Commonwealth Forum of National Human Rights Institutions, 'Kigali Declaration Moving from aspiration to action to prevent and eliminate child, early and forced marriage in the Commonwealth', 6 May 2015.

248 UN Committee on the Rights of the Child, General Comment No. 4, Adolescent health and development in the context of the Convention on the Rights of the Child, 1 July 2003, para 20.

249 Information provided to the NIHRC on request from the NI Statistics and Research Agency.

250 UN Committee on the Rights of the Child, Concluding Observations on the Fifth Periodic Report of the United Kingdom of Great Britain and NI, CRC/C/GBR/CO/5, UN CRC, 12 July 2016, para 19.

Human trafficking

The National Referral Mechanism is a framework operated by the National Crime Agency for identifying victims of human trafficking or modern slavery and ensuring they receive the appropriate support. During 2015, 53 potential victims of human trafficking were referred from NI. This figure included: 20 adult males; 20 adult females; eight boys; and, five girls.[251] Labour exploitation was the primary reason for referral, comprising 58 per cent of the referrals; while 22 per cent were referred for sexual exploitation; six per cent for domestic servitude; and another 13 per cent referred as unknown exploitation type.[252]

The Human Trafficking and Exploitation (Criminal Justice and Support for Victims) Act (NI) 2015 places a requirement on the Department of Justice to produce an annual strategy to address offences related to slavery, servitude and forced or compulsory labour and human trafficking. In furtherance of this obligation the Department of Justice published a draft strategy for consultation in July 2016.[253] The Commission responded to the consultation advising that the strategy would be strengthened by the inclusion of concrete and measurable outcomes, accompanied by additional proposals for how such outcomes are to be time-bound and effectively monitored and evaluated.[254] The Commission further advised that, in order to embed a human rights-based approach the Department should commit itself within the strategy to taking action consistent with international human rights standards, particularly those protecting the principles of non-refoulement and extraterritoriality.[255] In particular the Commission advised that, in line with the 2015 Act, regulations governing the appointment of independent guardians to assist, represent and support children who are believed to be victims of trafficking should be introduced.[256]

The finalised strategy is awaited.

251 National Crime Agency, National Referral Mechanism Statistics - End of Year Summary 2015, 11/02/2016, see Annex B.

252 National Crime Agency, National Referral Mechanism Statistics - End of Year Summary 2015, 11/02/2016, see Annex B.

253 Department of Justice, Draft NI Human Trafficking and Modern Slavery Strategy 2016/17, 1 July 2016.

254 NIHRC, Submission to Department of Justice consultation on a draft Human Trafficking and Modern Slavery Strategy, September 2016, para 2.7.

255 NIHRC, Submission to Department of Justice consultation on a draft Human Trafficking and Modern Slavery Strategy, September 2016, para 27.

256 NIHRC, Submission to Department of Justice consultation on a draft Human Trafficking and Modern Slavery Strategy, September 2016, para 4.8.

Right to fair trial and the administration of justice

ICCPR	Article 14 Article 15 Article 16
ECHR	Article 6 Article 7
CFREU	Article 47

Avoidable delay

In 2015 the UN Human Rights Committee recommended the introduction of:

concrete measures to reduce avoidable delays in the criminal justice system in NI, including by introducing custodial time limits.[257]

Custodial time limits were first introduced to England and Wales in 1991.[258] The Criminal Justice Inspector for NI has stated that failure to introduce statutory custodial time limits in NI, 'consigns the justice process here to continuing unacceptable delay in processing cases'.[259]

In 2016 the Department of Justice consulted on possible amendments to the Criminal Justice (NI) Order 2003 to strengthen the legislative basis for the introduction of a Statutory Time Limit scheme. The consultation invited views on options for the length and trigger for the time limit. The Commission has highlighted to officials the extent of delays within the criminal justice system and the need to address the recommendation of the UN Human Rights Committee.

In March 2016 prisoners held on remand accounted for just over 28 per cent of the overall prison population. This is an increase of around 5 per cent from the previous year.[260]

Witness charter

On the 5th July 2016, Justice Minister, Claire Sugden launched a public consultation on a Charter setting out the entitlements, services and support that a witness to a crime should expect from the criminal justice system.[261]

In correspondence to the Department of Justice the Commission welcomed the publication of the draft Witness Charter. The Commission advised that the Charter should make further reference to the provision of support to vulnerable witnesses, in particular those at risk. The Commission further advised that the Charter should recognise the obligation to ensure the best interests of any child witness is given paramount consideration and to ensure witnesses with a disability are able to access justice on an equal basis to anyone else, in line with CRPD Article 13.

257 UN Human Rights Committee, Concluding observations on the seventh periodic report of the United Kingdom of Great Britain and Northern Ireland, CCPR/C/GBR/CO/7, UN HRC, July 2015, para 22.

258 Fiona O'Connell, 'Statutory Time Limits', NI Assembly Research 125-12, 31 March 2012.

259 Official Report (Hansard) Session: 2013/2014 Date: 25 June 2014.

260 NI Prison Service, 'Analysis of NIPS Prison Population from 01/01/2015 to 31/03/2016', June 2016.

261 https://www.justice-ni.gov.uk/news/justice-minister-launches-witness-charter-consultation; Draft Witness Charter Consultation https://www.justice-ni.gov.uk/consultations/consultation-draft-witness-charter

🔴 Compensation for a miscarriage of justice

The Anti-social Behaviour, Crime and Policing Act 2014[262] redefined the test for a miscarriage of justice to require an applicant who has been wrongfully imprisoned to prove his or her innocence of a crime in order to obtain compensation.[263] This new test applies for all offences in England and Wales and for offences related to terrorism in NI. The new test is contained within s.133(1ZA) of the Criminal Justice Act 1988.

The Commission had previously advised that this approach was a disproportionate limitation of the ICCPR, Article 14(6), which states:

[w]hen a person has by a final decision been convicted of a criminal offence and when subsequently his conviction has been reversed, or he has been pardoned, on the ground that a new or newly discovered fact shows conclusively that there has been a miscarriage of justice, the person who has suffered punishment as a result of such conviction shall be compensated according to law, unless it is proved that the non-disclosure of the unknown fact in time is wholly or partly attributed to him.[264]

Prior to the introduction of the 2014 Act Lord Phillips in a legal judgement observed that:

The travaux [to the ICCPR] clearly demonstrate that the parties intended article 14(6) to cover the situation where a newly discovered fact demonstrated conclusively that the defendant was innocent of the crime of which he had been convicted. They were not, however, prepared to agree an interpretation which restricted the ambit of article 14(6) to this situation.[265]

Noting that the UN Human Rights Committee General Comment on Article 14 does not define the term 'miscarriage of justice', the Commission updated the Committee on the 2014 Act and requested its views.[266]

The Committee recommended that the UK:

Review the new test for a miscarriage of justice with a view to ensuring its compatibility with article 14, para. 6, of the Covenant.[267]

In April 2016 the England & Wales Court of Appeal considered an application that s.133(1ZA) was unlawful, as it was contrary to the presumption of innocence within article 6(2) ECHR. Rejecting the application the Court of Appeal ruled:

The critical reason why section 133 is not incompatible with article 6(2) is that, as the Divisional Court said, it does not require the applicant to prove his innocence generally. The key issue for the purpose of establishing eligibility for compensation under section 133 is the effect of the new or newly discovered fact which led to the conviction being quashed on appeal…. The fact that the Secretary of State is not persuaded beyond reasonable doubt by a new or newly discovered fact that an applicant is innocent does not entail that the Secretary of State casts doubt on his innocence generally. He is merely saying that the applicant's innocence has not been proved by the new or newly discovered fact.[268]

At the time of writing an appeal to the Supreme Court is under consideration.

---

262 Anti-social Behaviour Crime and Policing Act 2014, c. 12.

263 The Anti-social Behaviour, Crime and Policing Act 2014 makes amendments to section 133 of the Criminal Justice Act 1988.

264 NIHRC, 'The 2013 Annual Statement: Human Rights in NI', 2013, p. 29.

265 R (on the application of Adams) (FC) (Appellant) v Secretary of State for Justice (Respondent) [2011] UKSC 18, para 21.

266 Human Rights Committee, General Comment No. 32, Article 14: Right to equality before courts and tribunals and to a fair trial, 2007.

267 UN Human Rights Committee, Concluding observations on the seventh periodic report of the United Kingdom of Great Britain and Northern Ireland, CCPR/C/GBR/CO/7, UN HRC, July 2015, para 22 (b).

268 The Queen, on the applications of Sam Hallam and Victor Nealon - and - the Secretary of State for Justice [2016] EWCA Civ 355.

Closed material proceedings

The Justice and Security Act 2013 makes provision for closed material proceedings in civil cases allowing for the introduction of sensitive security evidence to proceedings involving the Government, without disclosure to the claimant.[269]

The UN Human Rights Committee has raised concerns regarding the 2013 Act and recommended that the UK:

> *Ensure that any restrictions or limitation to fair trial guarantees on the basis of national security grounds, including the use of closed material procedures, are fully compliant with its obligations under the Covenant, particularly that the use of closed material procedures in cases involving serious human rights violations do not create obstacles to the establishing of State responsibility and accountability as well as compromise the right of victims to a fair trial and an effective remedy.*[270]

The Commission continues to monitor the use of closed material procedures.

Access to justice

In 2015 the Commission advised the Department of Justice on proposals to reform the scope of civil legal aid in NI. The Department of Justice had sought views on re-structuring legal aid in private law children order cases to facilitate resolution, minimise conflict and produce sustainable solutions for all parties. The proposals included, limiting access to legal aid in such cases or removing them from scope entirely.[271]

In its advice, the Commission referred to the CRC General Comment 12 which recognises that:

> *all legislation on separation and divorce has to include the right of the child to be heard by decision makers and in mediation processes.*[272]

The Commission also referred to the experience of England and Wales where private law children order cases have been removed completely from the scope of civil legal aid, resulting in a significant increase in the number of litigants in persons before the court.[273]

Following the consultation, the Department of Justice reported that private law children order cases would not be removed from the scope of civil legal aid. The Commission has continued to engage with Department of Justice officials throughout 2016. The Commission is a member of a reference group chaired by Lord Justice Gillen to review civil and family justice.

In September 2016 the Commission and the Ulster University, School of Law commenced a research project on the needs of litigants in person including a human rights analysis of the circumstances in which representation is required in civil cases.[274]

---

269 Section 12 (1) of the Justice and Security Act 2013 requires the Secretary of State to prepare an annual report on the use of the closed material procedure under section 6 of the Act. Report on use of closed material procedure (from 25 June 2014 to 24 June 2015), October 2015, records that 9 applications for a declaration that a CMP application may be made in proceedings during the reporting period were made by the Secretary of State and two were made by the Chief Constable of the PSNI.

270 UN Human Rights Committee, Concluding observations on the seventh periodic report of the United Kingdom of Great Britain and Northern Ireland, CCPR/C/GBR/CO/7, UN HRC, July 2015, para 22.

271 Department of Justice, 'Scope of Civil Legal Aid' November 2014 – January 2015; See further NIHRC, 'Submission to Department of Justice consultation on the scope of civil legal aid', January 2015.

272 UN Committee on the Rights of the Child, General Comment No. 12 The right of the child to be heard, July 2009, para 51 – 52.

273 NIHRC, 'Submission to the Department of Justice Consultation on the Scope of Civil Legal Aid', January 2015, para 7.3.

274 UU/NIHRC Press Release, 'New research to uncover impact of going to court without a lawyer', 18 October 2016

Age of criminal responsibility

The age of criminal responsibility remains at ten years old in NI, as in England and Wales. Whilst it remains at eight in Scotland, the Criminal Justice and Licensing (Scotland) Act 2010 renders any prosecution of a child under twelve incompetent.[275]

In 2016 the UN CRC Committee once again recommended that the UK:

Raise the minimum age of criminal responsibility in accordance with acceptable international standards.[276]

The Commission has repeatedly advised that the minimum age of criminal responsibility should be raised to at least twelve in line with international human rights standards.[277] In correspondence to the Commission the Minister of Justice, Claire Sugden has indicated that due to a lack of cross party support for any increase in the age of criminal responsibility proposals for reform of the law is unlikely. However the Minister has identified the removal of children from the formal criminal justice system as a matter of priority.

Public Services Ombudsman

The Public Services Ombudsman Act (NI) 2016 received royal assent on 19 February 2016. The Act makes provision for the appointment, independence and investigative procedures of the Public Services Ombudsman.

The Act is a welcome development. The Act makes provision for the Ombudsman to consult and cooperate with the Commission, amongst other bodies.[278]

---

275 Criminal Justice and Licensing (Scotland) Act 2010, s. 52.

276 UN Committee on the Rights of the Child, Concluding Observations on the Fifth Periodic Report of the United Kingdom of Great Britain and NI, CRC/C/GBR/CO/5, UN CRC, 12 July 2016, para 79.

277 UN Committee on the Rights of the Child, Concluding observations: United Kingdom of Great Britain and Northern Ireland, CRC/C/GBR/CO/4, UN CRC, 2008; UN Committee on the Rights of the Child, Concluding observations: United Kingdom of Great Britain and Northern Ireland, CRC/C/15/Add 188, UN CRC, 2002; UN Committee on the Rights of the Child, Concluding Observations on the United Kingdom of Great Britain and Northern Ireland's initial report, CRC/C/15/Add 34, UN CRC, 15 February 1995.

278 Public Services Ombudsman Act (Northern Ireland) 2016, Section 52.

Right to private and family life

ICCPR	Article 17 Article 23
CRPD	Article 19 Article 22
ECHR	Article 8 Article 12
CFREU	Article 7 Article 8 Article 9
CRC	Article 16 Article 20 Article 21
ICESCR	Article 10 (1)

Alternative care arrangements for children

In 2016 the UN CRC Committee raised concern at the increase in the number of children in care throughout the UK:

Cases where early intervention measures have not been carried out in a timely manner, parents have not been provided with adequate family support and the best interests of the child have not been properly assessed in the decision of taking a child into care. Children have reportedly been removed from their biological families owing to the family's economic situation or because a foster family may provide a more beneficial environment for the child. [279]

The Commission published a report in 2015 entitled 'Alternative Care and Children's Rights in NI'.[280] This report made 29 recommendations and highlighted shortcomings in the provision of suitable and stable care placements for children in care.

In July 2016 the Department of Health published a statistical bulletin on the experiences of children in care in the financial year 2014/15.[281] The bulletin indicates a reduction in the proportion of children in care who had experienced a placement change in year; with 82 percent experiencing no placement change, up from 81 percent in 2013/2014. However in terms of outcomes for children in care only 66 per cent of children in care achieved one or more GCSEs in 2014/15 compared to 73 per cent the previous year. In contrast close to 100 per cent of the general school population achieved one or more GCSEs in 2014/15. Furthermore of children looked after aged ten and over at 30 September 2015, eight per cent (97) had been cautioned or convicted of an offence whilst in care during the year.[282] The equivalent proportion for England was three percentage points lower.

The Children's Services Co-operation Act (NI) 2015 received royal assent in December 2015. The Act places a statutory obligation on certain public authorities and other persons to contribute to the well-being of children and young persons and obligates the NI Executive to adopt a children and young

---

279 UN Committee on the Rights of the Child, Concluding Observations on the Fifth Periodic Report of the United Kingdom of Great Britain and NI, CRC/C/GBR/CO/5, UN CRC, 12 July 2016.

280 NIHRC, 'Alternative Care and Children's Rights in Northern Ireland', August 2015.

281 DHSSPS, Publication of the statistical bulletin 'Children in Care in NI 2014/15', 28th July 2016.

282 DHSSPS, Children in Care in NI 2014/15: Statistical Bulletin, 28th July 2016, para 8.1.

people strategy. Throughout 2016 the NI Executive has been developing a children and young people strategy.

In year the Commission advised the UN CRC Committee that the Adoption (NI) Order 1987 is out dated and is potentially out of step with various pieces of recent domestic equality legislation and the ECHR.[283] In addition, the Children (NI) Order 1995 is similarly outdated and has not integrated many developments which have taken place in corresponding legislation for England & Wales. The UN CRC Committee recommended that the State Party:

Expedite the approval and enactment of the Adoption and Children Bill in NI.

In October 2016 the Minister for Health informed the NI Assembly that:

An Adoption and Children Bill has been drafted. It is principally intended to modernise the legal framework for adoption in the North and place children's welfare at the centre of the adoption decision-making processes. The current law on adoption is the Adoption Order 1987. It is based on English legislation drafted in the early 1970s and therefore reflects practice that is effectively 40 years old. The Bill will deliver a framework for adoption that is more consistent with the principles and provisions of the Children Order 1995 and international human rights requirements.[284]

The Children (NI) Order 1995 makes provision for a child to be held in secure accommodation, meaning accommodation provided for the purpose of restricting liberty, under strict circumstances.[285] The Commission's 2015 Report identified that whilst Children Order Guidance and Regulations emphasise that secure accommodation should be used only as a measure of last resort concerns were raised as to whether, in practice, this is always the case.

In 2016 the UN CRC Committee recommended that the State Party:

Ensure that secure accommodation in Northern Ireland is only used as a measure of last resort and for the shortest possible period of time, address the reasons for repeated or lengthy stays in such accommodation and develop alternatives to secure accommodation.[286]

🟠 Stop and search

The Commission has previously referred to the NI Policing Board recommendation of 2013 that the Police Service NI, as soon as reasonably practicably, consider how it records the community background of all persons stopped and searched under powers contained within the Terrorism Act 2000 and within the Justice and Security (NI) Act 2007.[287]

In 2015 the UN Human Rights Committee called for implementation:

as a matter of priority [of], the recommendation of the Policing Board to the Police Service of NI concerning the inclusion in the Police Service NI's recording form of community background of persons stopped and searched under the Justice and Security (NI) Act 2007.[288]

283 NIHRC, Submission to the UN Committee on the Rights of the Child 72nd Session on the Fifth Periodic Report of the United Kingdom of Great Britain and Northern Ireland on compliance with the UN Convention on the Rights of the Child, 15 April 2016.

284 Adoption Legislation Oral Answers to Questions — Health – in the Northern Ireland Assembly at 2:15 pm on 18th October 2016.

285 The Children (NI) Order 1995, Article 44.

286 UN Committee on the Rights of the Child, Concluding Observations on the Fifth Periodic Report of the United Kingdom of Great Britain and NI, CRC/C/GBR/CO/5, UN CRC, 12 July 2016, para 53.

287 NI Policing Board, 'Human Rights Thematic Review on the use of police powers to stop and search and stop and question under the Terrorism Act 2000 and the Justice and Security (NI) Act 2007', October 2013.

288 UN Human Rights Committee, Concluding observations on the seventh periodic report of the United Kingdom of Great Britain and Northern Ireland, CCPR/C/GBR/CO/7, UN HRC, July 2015, para. 11(b).

The Police Service NI has developed a methodology for recording the community background of persons stopped and searched under the Terrorism Act 2000 and the Justice and Security (NI) Act 2007. This methodology was piloted for three months in Derry/Londonderry and Strabane from December 2015 to February 2016. The results of the pilot have been shared with the Policing Board Performance Committee and with the Commission. Publication of an evaluation report is awaited.

Housing (Anti-social Behaviour) Act 2016

In 2014 the Commission advised the Department of Social Development (now Department of Communities) on measures proposed to tackle anti-social behaviour in social housing.[289] The Department introduced the Housing (Anti-social Behaviour) Bill in 2015. The Bill, inter alia, provides a legal basis for the sharing of information in relation to anti-social behaviour.[290]

The Commission raised a number of issues on the breadth of the provisions under Clause 2; in particular, that the Bill may not meet the proportionality test under Article 8 of the ECHR in relation to the definition of 'person', 'relevant information', and the definition of 'relevant purpose'.[291]

The Commission recognised the need for appropriate powers for the Department of Social Development, NI Housing Executive and for housing associations to be able to access information to enable them to discharge their responsibilities fairly and effectively. However, it considered the phrasing in the Bill to have been drafted in very broad terms and questioned the proportionality of the proposed interference with the right to private and family life, protected by Article 8 of the ECHR.[292]

The Department, examining the issue further, assured the Committee that the definitions within the Bill are limited to information and purposes which are required for tackling anti-social behaviour. They confirmed that the definition of 'person' is as set out in the Interpretation Act (NI) 1954.[293] Given these assurances the Committee was content with the Department's explanation and that the Bill met the proportionality test under Article 8 of the ECHR.

Environmental Regulation

The Environmental Better Regulation Act (NI) 2016 received royal assent in April 2016. Part Two of the Act has been brought into effect.[294] The Act, inter alia, provides for a review of powers of entry and associated powers relating to the protection of the environment and for the repeal or rewriting of such powers and for safeguards in relation to them. The Commission broadly welcomes the Act and welcomes that amendments were made at the Committee stage implementing the majority of the Commission's recommendations,[295] including defining 'home' and 'moveable property' to prevent potential discrimination against the traveller community.[296]

The Commission notes that the Act is an enabling piece of legislation which grants the Department of Agriculture, Environment and Rural Affairs the power to introduce secondary legislation. Currently there is no secondary legislation in force under the Act, and the Commission understands that although preliminary scoping work has begun on subordinate legislation in respect of the

289 DSD, 'NI Proposed Housing (Anti-Social Behaviour) Bill (NI) A Consultation Document', 2013.

290 Bill 58/11-16.

291 NIHRC, 'Response of the Northern Ireland Human Rights Commission to the Housing (Amendment) Bill. NIA Bill 58/11-16', September 2015

292 NIHRC, 'Response of the Northern Ireland Human Rights Commission to the Housing (Amendment) Bill. NIA Bill 58/11-16', September 2015, para 4.17.

293 NI Assembly, Committee for Social Development, 'Report on the Housing (Amendment) Bill NIA 58/11-16' NIA 269/11-16, January 2016.

294 The Environmental Better Regulation (2016 Act) (Commencement No. 1) Order (Northern Ireland) 2016, Made 15th April 2016, available at http://www.legislation.gov.uk/nisr/2016/212/contents/made

295 Committee for the Environment, Report on the Environmental Better Regulation Bill, (NIA 55/11-16), Report: NIA 277/11-16 Committee for the Environment, November 2015, available at http://www.niassembly.gov.uk/globalassets/committee-blocks/environment/final-agreed-report-on-environmental-better-regulation-bill.pdf. See further Explanatory Notes Environmental Better Regulation Act 2016, Clause 13, available at http://www.legislation.gov.uk/nia/2016/13/notes/division/4/2.

296 Committee for the Environment, Report on the Environmental Better Regulation Bill, (NIA 55/11-16), Report: NIA 277/11-16 Committee for the Environment, November 2015, available at http://www.niassembly.gov.uk/globalassets/committee-blocks/environment/final-agreed-report-on-environmental-better-regulation-bill.pdf. See further Explanatory Notes Environmental Better Regulation Act 2016, Clause 13, available at http://www.legislation.gov.uk/nia/2016/13/notes/division/4/2.

environmental permitting system, any resulting regulations are unlikely to come into force in the near future. Any future regulations will have human rights implications, but the Act itself is consistent with the state's human rights obligations.

There is an intrinsic link between the environment and the realisation of human rights. The rights to health, water, food, housing, life and privacy, all place obligations on the NI Executive and Departments to take actions to prevent adverse environmental impact upon the individual. The Commission continues to note that NI is the only part of the UK not to have an independent environmental regulator.

Health and Social Care (Control of Data Processing) Act 2016

The Health and Social Care (Control of Data Processing) Act 2016 received royal assent on 11 April 2016. On implementation the Act will provide a statutory framework, including safeguards, which will enable the use of health and social care information for the benefit of health and social care research.

The Commission broadly welcomed the then Bill and provided specific advice to the NI Assembly Health Committee.[297] The Commission advised that the European Court of Human Rights has held that the protection of medical data falls within the ambit of the right to private and family life, protected by Article 8 of the ECHR.[298] The Commission further advised that laws which interfere with the right to private and family life must be formulated with sufficient precision to afford adequate legal protection against arbitrariness and indicate with sufficient clarity the scope of discretion conferred on the competent authorities.[299]

The Commission advised that the Department must establish a Committee to authorise the processing of confidential information. The Commission's advice was reflected in the Act.[300]

---

297   NIHRC, 'Advice on the Health and Social Care (Control of Data Processing)' NI Bill 52/11-16.
298   NIHRC, 'Advice on the Health and social Care (Control of Data processing)' NIA Bill 53/11-16, para 13.
299   NIHRC, 'Advice on the Health and Social Care (Control of Data Processing)' NIA Bill 52/11-16, para 14.
300   Health and Social Care (Control of Data Processing) Act (Northern Ireland) 2016, s 2(1).

Freedom of religion and belief, expression, association and right to participate in public and political life

ICCPR	Article 18 Article 19 Article 20 Article 21 Article 22 Article 25
ECHR	Article 9 Article 10 Article 11 Protocol 1 Article 3
CFREU	Article 10 Article 11 Article 12
CRC	Article 13 Article 14 Article 15
CEDAW	Article 3
CRPD	Article 19 Article 21 Article 29

Parades and protests

The Commission has previously referred to the call by the UN Special Rapporteur on Peaceful Assembly, Parades and Association for 'political resolution of the issues – such as parades, flags and emblems – that still make the enjoyment of freedom of peaceful assembly problematic in NI'.[301] The Stormont House Agreement proposed that responsibility for parades and related protests should, in principle, be devolved to the NI Assembly.[302] It also proposed that the Office of Legislative Counsel, working in conjunction with the Office of the First Minister and Deputy First Minister (now the Executive Office), should produce a range of options on how the remaining key issues which include the Code of Conduct, criteria and accountability could be addressed in legislation. The Office of the First Minister and Deputy First Minister (now the Executive Office) was to bring forward proposals to the NI Executive by June 2015.[303]

In 2015/16 the Parades Commission were notified of 2,851 loyalist/unionist, 219 nationalist/republican and 1,960 other parades. The vast majority of parades passed off peacefully.[304] In September 2016 an agreement was reached regarding a long running protest which began after a Parades Commission determination not to allow the return leg of an Orange Order parade to pass a section of the Crumlin Road in 2013.[305] The agreement led to the removal of a protest camp established at Twadell Avenue.

---

301 Report of the Special Rapporteur on the rights to freedom of peaceful assembly and of association, Maina Kiai, on his mission to the United Kingdom (14-23 January 2013) A/HRC/23/39/Add.1, para 96. Available at: http://www.ohchr.org/Documents/HRBodies/HRCouncil/RegularSession/Session23/A-HRC-23-39-Add1_en.pdf

302 Stormont House Agreement, 2014, para 17.

303 Stormont House agreement, 2014, para 18.

304 Parades Commission for Northern Ireland, 'Annual Report and Financial Statements for the year ended 31 March 2016', House of Commons, 2016, p. 9. https://www.paradescommission.org/getmedia/0022c84a-6b95-4239-ad80-3cdc1da26a49/NorthernIrelandParadesCommission.aspx

305 BBC News NI, 'Twaddell: Agreement reached over long-running parade dispute', 24 September 2016.

The Commission has consistently advised all those participating or responsible for the regulation of parades and protests that a broad range of human rights and state obligations are engaged. Human rights law, in particular the jurisprudence of the European Court of Human Rights, is a valuable resource for resolving disputes relating to parades, protests and related adjudicative processes. Furthermore, it is sufficiently flexible to accommodate alternative mechanisms for resolution which seek to develop innovative compromise agreements.[306]

Participation of women in public and political life

In October 2014 the results of an independent assessment into gender equality at the executive level in the public sector in NI identified 'a significant degree of inequality in the gender composition at executive level of the NI public sector: males and females holding 70.8 per cent and 29.2 per cent of all executive positions respectively'.[307] The research report identified a number of barriers to career progression amongst women in the civil service including: those related to caring responsibilities, a lack of recognition of work life balance, long hours' culture and exclusion from informal networks of communication.[308]

There are 297 female judicial office holders in NI representing 43 per cent of the total.[309] Female judicial office holders have traditionally been broadly concentrated amongst the lower ranking judicial posts.[310] For the first time in the history of the NI judiciary two women, Denise McBride QC and Siobhan Keegan QC, were appointed in 2015 as High Court judges.[311]

The Sex Discrimination (NI) Order 1976, section 43A allows political parties to take positive measures to reduce inequality between men and women elected to Parliament, the NI Assembly, District Councils and the European Parliament.[312] The Commission notes, however, that this provision has not been utilised in NI and women continue to be under-represented in political life (albeit there are variations in the patterns of representation depending on the particular office concerned).

In 2015 the UN Human Rights Committee recommended:

that all existing and future gender equality strategies and policies, including the Gender Equality Strategy for NI, identify and address effectively the barriers hindering women's access to high positions in the civil service and in the judiciary.[313]

In 2016 the Commission advised the UN ICESCR Committee that women generally continue to be under-represented in political life.[314] Following the 2016 elections, female representation at the NI Assembly is 27 per cent[315] and 21 per cent of the Assembly's Committee Chairpersons are female.[316] There have been positive steps forward. In January 2016, Arlene Foster, MLA became the First Minister of NI, the first woman to hold this office.[317] The NI Assembly saw an increase of 50 per cent

306 NIHRC, Parades and Protests in Northern Ireland, 2013, p. 2. http://www.nihrc.org/uploads/publications/110720_NIHRC_Parades_and_Protests_in_NI_REPORT_cover_inners_Single_Col_V3_LOW.pdf

307 Professor Joan Ballantine, Dr Graeme Banks, Professor Kathryn Haynes, Dr Melina Manochin, Mr Tony Wall, 'An Investigation of Gender Equality Issues at the Executive Level in Northern Ireland Public Sector Organisations', October 2014.

308 Professor Joan Ballantine, Dr Graeme Banks, Professor Kathryn Haynes, Dr Melina Manochin, Mr Tony Wall, 'An Investigation of Gender Equality Issues at the Executive Level in Northern Ireland Public Sector Organisations', October 2014, p. 118.

309 NIJAC, 'The Judiciary Northern Ireland 2014 Equality Monitoring Report', April 2014.

310 NIJAC, 'The Judiciary Northern Ireland 2014 Equality Monitoring Report,' April 2014; See further, QUB, 'Rewarding Merit in Judicial Appointments', January 2013.

311 https://www.courtsni.gov.uk/en-GB/AboutUs/OrganisationalStructure/Pages/Judiciary-of-Northern-Ireland.aspx

312 The Sex Discrimination (Northern Ireland) Order 1976, section 43A. The provisions have been extended to 2030 by section 105(3) of the Equality Act 2010.

313 UN Human Rights Committee, Concluding observations on the seventh periodic report of the United Kingdom of Great Britain and Northern Ireland, CCPR/C/GBR/CO/7, UN HRC, July 2015, para 12.

314 NIHRC, 'Submission to the UN Committee on Economic, Social and Cultural Rights 58th Session on the Sixth Periodic Report of the United Kingdom's Compliance with ICESCR', 2016, pp. 38-40.

315 http://aims.niassembly.gov.uk/mlas/statistics.aspx

316 http://www.niassembly.gov.uk/assembly-business/committees/chairperson-liaison-group/membership/

317 The Guardian, Arlene Foster becomes Northern Ireland's First Minister, 11 January 2016.

in the number of women MLAs, from 20 in 2011 to 30 in 2016 elections.[318] The NI Executive is also 41 per cent female.[319] Female representation within the UK Parliament is 11 per cent.[320] At a local government level, 25 per cent of councillors elected in 2014 were women.[321]

Within its 2016 concluding observations on the UK, the UN ICESCR Committee noted its concern at the persistent under-representation of women in decision-making positions in the public and private sectors. The UN ICESCR Committee recommended that the State party:

intensify its efforts to increase the level of representation of women in decision-making positions, in both the public and private sectors.[322]

Blasphemy

The UN Human Rights Committee has elaborated on the ICCPR, Article 19 on the right to freedom of expression and opinion by way of a General Comment stating that:

Prohibitions of displays of lack of respect for a religion or other belief system, including blasphemy laws, are incompatible with the Covenant, except in the specific circumstances envisaged in article 20, paragraph 2, of the Covenant.[323] Such prohibitions must also comply with the strict requirements of article 19, paragraph 3, as well as such articles as 2, 5, 17, 18 and 26. Thus, for instance, it would be impermissible for any such laws to discriminate in favour of or against one or certain religions or belief systems, or their adherents over another, or religious believers over non-believers. Nor would it be permissible for such prohibitions to be used to prevent or punish criticism of religious leaders or commentary on religious doctrine and tenets of faith.[324]

In its 2008 report on the UK the UN Human Rights Committee welcomed the introduction of the Criminal Justice and Immigration Act 2008 abolishing the common law offence of blasphemy in England and Wales.[325] During the passage of the 2008 Act the House of Lords debated extending the Act to include NI.[326] The Lords noted that blasphemy was part of the common law of Ireland but that it was unclear if the common law precedent survived the disestablishment of the Church of Ireland by the Irish Church Act 1869.[327] Furthermore the Lords noted that there was no reported blasphemy prosecution in the period between 1855 and the creation of the independent state of Ireland and that the offence had not been prosecuted since the establishment of NI.[328]

Since the devolution of policing and justice powers to the NI Assembly, the NI Executive has not undertaken a review of blasphemy laws to determine if the common law offence is still in place. In 2016 the Commission raised this issue with the UN Human Rights Council.[329]

318 BBC News, 'NI Assembly election: Number of women MLAs increases by 50%', 9 May 2016. Available at: http://www.bbc.co.uk/news/election-2016-northern-ireland-36542522.

319 http://aims.niassembly.gov.uk/mlas/ministers.aspx

320 http://www.parliament.uk/mps-lords-and-offices/mps/?search_term=Northern+Ireland

321 North South Inter-parliamentary Association, Briefing Paper for the Seventh Meeting of the North-south Inter-Parliamentary Association: Women in Public Life, North South Inter-parliamentary Association, 27 November 2015.

322 UN Committee on Economic, Social and Cultural Rights, Concluding observations on the sixth periodic report of the United Kingdom of Great Britain and Northern Ireland E/C.12/GBR/CO/6, UN Economic and Social Council, 14 July 2016, para 17(d).

323 ICCPR article 20, paragraph 2 states 'Any advocacy of national, racial or religious hatred that constitutes incitement to discrimination, hostility or violence shall be prohibited by law'.

324 UN Human Rights Committee, General Comment 34 on Article 19: Freedoms of opinion and expression, CCPR/C/GC/34. 12 September 2011. Available at: http://www2.ohchr.org/english/bodies/hrc/docs/gc34.pdf

325 UN Human Rights Committee, Concluding Observations of the Human Rights Committee on the sixth Periodic Report of the United Kingdom of Great Britain and Northern Ireland, CCPR/C/GBR/CO/6, UN HRC, July 2008.

326 Hansard script Wednesday 28 Oct 2009 Volume No. 713 Part No. 125.

327 House of Lords, 'Religious Offences in England and Wales - First Report', HL Paper 95 -1, 10 April 2003, see appendix 5.

328 Ibid.

329 NIHRC, 'Submission to UN Human Rights Council's Universal Periodic Review of the UK' September 2016

⬤ Defamation

In 2008 the UN Human Rights Committee raised concerns that the:

practical application of the law of libel [in the UK] has served to discourage critical media reporting on matters of serious public interest, adversely affecting the ability of scholars and journalists to publish their work, including through the phenomenon known as "libel tourism."… The State party should re-examine its technical doctrines of libel law, and consider the utility of a so-called "public figure" exception, requiring proof by the plaintiff of actual malice in order to go forward on actions concerning reporting on public officials and prominent public figures…[330]

The Defamation Act 2013, elsewhere in the UK to some extent, addressed this recommendation. However the Act does not include NI.

In July 2016 the Department of Finance published the report of Dr Andrew Scott on reform to the law of defamation in NI. The Report recommends that,

to a significant extent, measures equivalent to the provisions of the Defamation Act 2013 should be introduced into NI law.[331]

The Report, in particular, recommended the introduction of a new defence of honest opinion, similar to section 3 of the Defamation Act 2013 with some additions.[332]

The Minister of Finance welcomed the publication of the report and stated:

This will help to inform the policy development process as we seek to ensure that a fair balance is maintained between the right to free speech and the right of the ordinary man and woman in the street, to protect their reputation.[333]

330 UN Human Rights Committee, Concluding Observations of the Human Rights Committee on the sixth Periodic Report of the United Kingdom of Great Britain and Northern Ireland, CCPR/C/GBR/CO/6, UN HRC, July 2008.

331 Dr Andrew Scott, ' Reform of Defamation Law in Northern Ireland: Recommendations to the Department of Finance', Department of Law, London School of Economics and Political Science, June 2016.

332 Dr Andrew Scott, ' Reform of Defamation Law in Northern Ireland: Recommendations to the Department of Finance', Department of Law, London School of Economics and Political Science, June 2016, paras 3.60 – 3.66

333 Department of Finance: Press Release, 'Ó Muilleoir announces publication of defamation report', 19 July 2016. https://www.finance-ni.gov.uk/news/o-muilleoir-announces-publication-defamation-report

Right to work and to just and favourable conditions of work

ICESCR	Article 6
	Article 7
CEDAW	Article 11
ESC	Article1
	Article 2
	Article 3
	Article 4
	Article 5
	Article 6
	Article 19
CFREU	Article 15

Accessible childcare

In its 2014 annual statement the Commission referred to the absence of a childcare strategy for NI.[334] In 2016 the NI Executive consulted on a draft strategy.[335] The Commission provided advice and recommended that the NI Executive introduce an adequately funded childcare strategy which ensures affordable and accessible childcare is available throughout NI.[336]

Officials from the Office of the First Minister and Deputy First Minister (now the Executive Office) briefed the Committee for First Minister and Deputy First Minister on the outcomes of the consultation on the draft Childcare Strategy in March 2016. The officials informed the Committee that the process of drafting would be completed in four to six weeks and would be signed off by the NI Executive after the NI Assembly elections in May. The work on the strategy will be taken over by the Department of Education under the transfer of functions.[337]

In April 2016, the Commission raised concerns with the UN ICESCR Committee about the accessibility of childcare in NI, particularly in relation to concerns regarding availability and affordability of childcare for certain groups. The Commission also noted that there is no statutory duty on public authorities to ensure adequate childcare unlike in the rest of the UK and that the draft Childcare Strategy for NI remained outstanding.[338]

The Commission advised the UN ICESCR Committee to recommend that the State party:

- *prioritises the urgent publication of a Childcare Strategy in NI and dedicates the necessary resources to ensure the availability of accessible and affordable childcare;*

- *ensures a model that operates outside traditional working hours to meet the needs of those working atypical shift patterns, as is the case for many parents in NI, including in particular BME parents.*[339]

---

334 NIHRC, 'The 2014 Annual statement: Human Rights in NI', December 2014, p. 43.

335 OFMDFM, 'A Ten Year Strategy for Affordable and Integrated Childcare 2015-2025', September 2015.

336 NIHRC, 'Response to the OFMDFM Consultation on a Ten Year Strategy for Affordable and Integrated Childcare 2015-2025', November 2015.

337 Briefing by OFMDFM officials to the Committee for OFMDFM, 2 March 2016, http://niassembly.tv/video/committee-office-first-minister-deputy-first-minister-meeting-02-march-2016/.

338 NIHRC, Submission to the UN Committee on Economic, Social and Cultural Rights 58th Session on the Sixth Periodic Report of the United Kingdom's Compliance with ICESCR, April 2016, paras 20.1- 20.4.

339 NIHRC, Submission to the UN Committee on Economic, Social and Cultural Rights 58th Session on the Sixth Periodic Report of the United Kingdom's Compliance with ICESCR, April 2016, p. 36.

The UN ICESCR Committee recommended that the State party increase its efforts to ensure the availability, accessibility and affordability of childcare services throughout the State party. The Committee also recommended that the State party review the system of shared parental leave and modify it with a view to improve the equal sharing of responsibilities within the family and in the society.[340]

In a response to an Assembly question in September 2016, the Minister for Education indicated that the strategy would be finalised 'in the coming months'.[341]

Armed Forces Covenant

Throughout 2016 the full implementation of the Armed Forces Covenant throughout NI has remained outstanding. The Commission has raised this issue since 2013. The NI Affairs Committee at Westminster announced its inquiry into the implementation of the Covenant in NI in 2012. The Committee reported that it had received mixed evidence about the level of progress on implementing the Armed Forces Covenant in NI, compared to other parts of the UK.[342] In particular, certain benefits were not available in NI, including improved access to in vitro fertilisation treatment, priority in accessing healthcare, additional priority in accessing social housing, schools and other educational entitlements.[343] However, the NI Affairs Committee also received evidence that indicated that local solutions could be found in most cases where the above differences affected the Armed Forces community and that there was no significant disadvantage to veterans who chose to settle in NI.

On 16 December 2014 the Secretary of State for Defence laid the 2014 'Annual Report on the Armed Forces Covenant' in HM Parliament. Whilst recording that the Armed Forces Covenant remained unimplemented in NI the report recorded that the Department of Social Development (now Department of Communities) had adopted the position that applicants for social housing or homelessness assistance must not be disadvantaged because of a background in the Armed Forces and developed a veterans' support forum.[344] The former Department of Social Development (now Department for Communities) issued guidance to the NI Housing Executive that former armed forces personnel are at particular risk of homelessness and rough sleeping and applications should be considered carefully to assess whether an applicant is vulnerable as a result of their service.[345] The Commission welcomed this initiative. In January 2015 the Minister of State, Ministry of Defence, stated that 'nearly all of the measures in the Covenant now extend to NI or will soon do so'.[346] A BBC Spotlight documentary in May 2015 reported that the greatest shortfall in treatment in NI was for those suffering from post-traumatic stress disorder.[347]

In January 2016, Gavin Robinson MP asked the Defence Secretary what proportion of the Armed Forces Covenant applies in NI. The Parliamentary Under-Secretary of State for Defence, Mark Lancaster MP noted the outcome of the Select Committee report in 2013 and acknowledged that the Covenant 'does not enjoy the same level of awareness or appreciation in NI'. Nevertheless, he stated that 'every effort is being made to implement the Covenant against the particular nuances of the Northern Irish political and legal environment'.[348]

---

340 UN Committee on Economic, Social and Cultural Rights, Concluding observations on the sixth periodic report of the United Kingdom of Great Britain and Northern Ireland E/C.12/GBR/CO/6, UN Economic and Social Council, 14 July 2016, para. 44.

341 AQW 2770/16-21, Ms Catherine Seeley.

342 Northern Ireland Affairs Committee, 'Implementation of the Armed Forces Covenant in Northern Ireland', First Report of session 2013/14 HC 51, 17th July 2013, p. 7.

343 Northern Ireland Affairs Committee, 'Implementation of the Armed Forces Covenant in Northern Ireland', First Report of session 2013/14 HC 51, 17th July 2013, p. 3.

344 Ministry of Defence, Armed Forces Covenant Annual Report 2014, December 2014.

345 Ministry of Defence, Armed Forces Covenant Annual Report 2014, December 2014, pp. 38-39.

346 UK Parliament, Armed Forces Covenant: Northern Ireland: Written question-220197, Answered on: 19th Jan 2015, Anna Soubry.

347 BBC Spotlight, 26th May 2015. See also BBC News, Captain Doug Beattie accuses government of 'abandoning' Northern Ireland military veterans,' 26th May 2015.

348 House of Commons, Armed Forces Covenant: Northern Ireland: Written Question 22172, 18 January 2016.

During the second reading of the Armed Forces Bill in the House of Lords in February 2016, the Minister of State at the Ministry of Defence, Earl Howe stated, in response to an intervention by Lord Empey that:

delivery of the covenant extends to the whole of the UK and that there is money to underpin that in NI… It is important that we continue to work together to ensure that there is universal support for the Armed Forces wherever they work and live, and that must extend to NI.[349]

In September 2016, Danny Kinahan MP asked the Defence Secretary what discussions he has had with the NI Executive on the appointment of a representative from NI to the Armed Forces Covenant Reference Group. The Parliamentary Under-Secretary of State responded that:

the Armed Forces Covenant is making a real difference in NI, where it is enshrined in law. Funding bids have been more successful there than in any other part of the UK – grants include £450,000 to Combat Stress to provide mental health support to veterans. There is an open invitation to the NI Executive to join the Covenant Reference Group. The Government wishes them to take a full and active part in the group, alongside the other Devolved Administrations. Whilst the NI Executive has not yet put forward a representative for the Covenant Reference Group, much useful and effective engagement takes place at Executive departmental level.[350]

The UN ICESCR Committee released General Comment 23 in April 2016 on the right to just and favourable conditions of work (Article 7 of the ICESCR) which states:

the enjoyment of the right to just and favourable conditions of work is a prerequisite for, and result of, the enjoyment of other Covenant rights, for example, the right to the highest attainable standard of physical and mental health, by avoiding occupational accidents and disease, and an adequate standard of living through decent remuneration.[351]

It was reported in October 2016 that increasing numbers of veterans were facing difficulties in accessing help to deal with mental health problems and there are ongoing problems with the implementation of the Armed Forces Covenant in NI.[352]

349   Earl Howe, HL Deb, 11 February 2016, c.2422.

350   Ministry of Defence written question, Armed Forces Covenant Reference Group: Northern Ireland, 44297,8 September 2016,

351   UN Committee on Economic, Social and Cultural Rights, General comment No. 23 (2016) on the right to just and favourable conditions of work E/C.12/GC/23, UN Economic and Social Council, 27 April 2016.

352   BBC News NI, "NI charity helps more than 100 army veterans who tried to take their own lives", 16 October 2016.

Right to an adequate standard of living and to social security

ICESCR	Article 7 Article 9 Article 11
CRC	Article 26 Article 27
CEDAW	Article 14
CRPD	Article 28
ESC	Article 12 Article 13 Article 14
CFREU	Article 15

Social security

In its previous annual statements the Commission reported on the advice provided to the NI Assembly in relation to the Welfare Reform Bill, which identified a number of potential consequential impacts on the protection of human rights.[353]

After the conclusion of political talks, agreement was reached in the 'Fresh Start Agreement' on a package of measures on welfare, paramilitarism and a commitment to a commencement date for the devolution of Corporation Tax.[354] The Executive agreed to allocate a total of £585 million from Executive funds over four years to top up the UK welfare arrangements in NI, with a review in 2018-19. The Executive also established a working group to bring forward recommendations on how to mitigate some of the adverse impacts of social security reform within the financial envelope available. The working group published its recommendations in January 2016 recommending a mitigation strategy with three strands: providing supplementary payments to carers, persons unable to work due to ill health, persons with disabilities and families; supporting and protecting claimants with independent advice; and ways to alleviate hardship as a result of Universal Credit. The First Minister of NI said that she would fully implement the recommendations made by the working group to mitigate the impact of social security reform.[355]

The NI Assembly passed a Legislative Consent Motion in November 2015 to allow Westminster to legislate for the introduction of welfare reform. The NI (Welfare Reform) Act 2015 was given royal assent on 25 November 2015 and the Welfare Reform (NI) Order 2015 was made in December 2015. The Act provided for an Order in Council for Westminster to legislate for welfare reform in NI, broadly equivalent to the reforms in the Welfare Reform Act 2012 and to confer a power on the Secretary of State or on a NI Department to make further provision by regulation or order. The introduction of social security reform in NI brought the regime of financial penalties to an end. There were also other developments at Westminster, some of which will have an adverse impact on NI. The Welfare Reform and Work Act 2016 contains provisions that extend to NI. These include provisions which freeze Child Benefit and tax credits for four tax years alongside changes to Universal Credit, including a less generous means testing arrangement withdrawing financial support much earlier and support for new claimants being restricted to cover the first two children only.

---

353   NIHRC, The 2012 Annual Statement: Human Rights in NI, December 2012.

354   Northern Ireland Executive, A Fresh Start: The Stormont Agreement and Implementation Plan, 17 November 2015, pp 22-23.

355   BBC News NI, NI Welfare Reform: Arlene Foster "will fully implement" welfare mitigation proposals, 22 January 2016.

The Housing Benefit (Amendment No.2) Regulations (NI) 2016 provide for deductions from a social rented sector working age claimant's eligible rent if they are deemed to be under-occupying their home and is due to commence on 23 January 2017. These regulations provide for limited protection from deductions by providing exemptions for an additional bedroom for children who cannot share due to severe disability, for persons who require overnight care, for certain qualifying parents approved to foster, and for adult children who are members of the armed forces and are deployed on operations.[356] The Welfare Supplementary Payment (Benefit Cap) Regulations (NI) 2016 provide for making mitigation payments on the reduction of the benefit cap. The Department for Communities has developed a composite Welfare Reform evaluation strategy to evaluate the key reforms as well as the associated mitigations.[357]

The Commission updated the UN ICESCR Committee on the changes to social security in April 2016. The UN ICESCR Committee made a number of recommendations to the UK Government on social security in its concluding observations. These included: review the entitlement conditions and reverse the cuts in social security benefits introduced by the Welfare Reform Act 2012 and the Welfare Reform and Work Act 2016; restore the link between the rates of State benefits and the costs of living and guarantee that all social security benefits provide a level of benefit sufficient to ensure an adequate standard of living, including access to health care, adequate housing and food; review the use of sanctions in relation to social security benefits and ensure they are used proportionately and are subject to prompt and independent dispute resolution mechanisms; and provide in its next report disaggregated data on the impact of social security reforms on women, children, persons with disabilities, low income families and families with two or more children.[358]

In November 2016 the UNCRPD Committee published a report of an inquiry into the UK. The Committee found that the cumulative impact of reforms to the social security system had resulted in grave or systematic violations of the rights of persons with disabilities.[359]

Social housing

Housing Supply

At March 2015, the total number of applicants on the social housing waiting list was 39,338. Of these applicants, 22,097 were in housing stress, where they had 30 or more points under the Common Selection Scheme. The number of properties allocated by the NI Housing Executive and Housing Associations to applicants on the waiting list who were not already social housing tenants was 8,129 in 2014-15. There were 2,763 allocations made by the NI Housing Executive and Housing Associations to tenants who had applied for a transfer from an existing tenancy.[360] There is an overall requirement of 190,000 new dwellings needed in NI between 2008 and 2025, an annual figure of 11,200.[361] Current targets fall significantly short of this.

The Social Housing Development Programme target for 2015/16 is to deliver 1,500 social homes (with aspiration to deliver 2000) with the remainder to be developed as affordable and private market housing.[362] The former Department of Social Development (now the Department for Communities) committed in the 'Facing the Future: Housing Strategy for NI 2012-2017' to ensuring access to decent affordable sustainable homes across all tenures and meet housing need and support the most

356 SR. No.258/2016.

357 AQW 2916/16-21, Mr Andy Allen.

358 UN Committee on Economic, Social and Cultural Rights, Concluding observations on the sixth periodic report of the United Kingdom of Great Britain and Northern Ireland E/C.12/GBR/CO/6, UN Economic and Social Council, 14 July 2016.

359 UNCRPD Committee Inquiry concerning the UK carried out by the Committee under article 6 of the Optional Protocol, 6 October 2016.

360 DSD, Northern Ireland Housing Statistics 2014-15, Analytical Services Unit, 17th November 2015, p. 42.

361 NIHE, NI Housing Market Review and Perspectives 2015-2018, 2015, p. 23.

362 Housing Supply Forum, Report and Recommendations: January 2016, p. 7.

vulnerable.[363] The Housing Supply Forum was established as a result of the strategy with a view to identifying ways of helping to increase housing supply in NI.[364]

The Housing Supply Forum published its report in January 2016, concluding that there were not enough homes being constructed in NI to meet demand.[365] The Forum made a number of recommendations, including issues such as: the completion of a mapping exercise, assessing demand and availability; and increased support and encouragement from Government for joint ventures between Housing Associations and private developers. It also recommended that powers be made available to the new local councils to enable sites to be developed for the benefit of the whole community and to ensure appropriate delivery of housing need.[366]

In 2016 the Commission highlighted to the UN ICESCR Committee the recommendations of the Housing Supply Forum in NI that concerted action should be was taken to increase housing supply to meet demand in NI within a reasonable and specified time-frame.[367]

The UN ICESCR Committee in the 2016 Concluding Observations urged the UK to:

adopt all necessary measures to address the housing deficit by ensuring a sufficient supply of housing, in particular social housing units, especially for the most disadvantaged and marginalised individuals and groups, including middle-and-low-income individuals and households, young people and persons with disabilities.[368]

Segregation

The Commission advised the UN ICESCR Committee in 2015 that due to the particular circumstances of NI, a high percentage of social housing stock is segregated, particularly in more urban areas. Research published by the NI Housing Executive in 2009 reported that based on the 2001 census, 91 per cent of social housing in Belfast NI Housing Executive estates were highly polarised, defined as having more than 80 per cent of one community or less than 20 per cent of one community in an estate.[369]

Research commissioned by the Equality Commission for NI found that in using data for all of NI, Catholic households waited longer than Protestant households to be allocated proportionately fewer homes, despite comprising a greater proportion of the waiting list and a greater proportion of applicants in housing stress.[370] The research noted that the situation is complex as spatial segregation declined from the period 2001 to 2011 when a growing middle ground was observed, i.e some people who may have identified as no religion, may have previously identified as Protestant in 2001.[371] This may have exaggerated Protestant decline in some wards and international migration may have bolstered the Catholic population in some formerly wholly Protestant wards.[372]

One of the key priorities under the 'Together Building a United Community Strategy' is the creation of new shared communities as the NI Life and Times Survey indicates that 82 per cent of respondents would prefer to live in a mixed neighbourhood and 87 per cent believe that better relations will come

---

363 DSD, Facing the Future: The Housing Strategy for NI 2012-17, 2012; DSD, Facing the Future: The Housing Strategy for Northern Ireland Action Plan Update: September 2015, 2015.

364 Housing Supply Forum, Report and Recommendations: January 2016.

365 Housing Supply Forum, Report and Recommendations: January 2016, p. 10.

366 Housing Supply Forum, Report and Recommendations: January 2016, pp. 13-19.

367 NIHRC, Submission to the UN Committee on Economic, Social and Cultural Rights 58th Session on the Sixth Periodic Report of the United Kingdom's Compliance with ICESCR, April 2016, pp. 53-55.

368 UN Committee on Economic, Social and Cultural Rights, Concluding observations on the sixth periodic report of the United Kingdom of Great Britain and Northern Ireland E/C.12/GBR/CO/6, UN Economic and Social Council, 14 July 2016, para 50(a).

369 Ian Shuttleworth and Christ Lloyd, Mapping Segregation in NI: NIHE Estates Outside Belfast, NIHE, 2009, p. 4.

370 Alison Wallace, Housing and Communities' Inequalities in Northern Ireland, CHP and University of York, 2015, p. 76.

371 Alison Wallace, Housing and Communities' Inequalities in Northern Ireland, CHP and University of York, 2015, p. 76.

372 Alison Wallace, Housing and Communities' Inequalities in Northern Ireland, CHP and University of York, 2015, p. 76.

about through more mixing. Two of the commitments under the strategy are the creation of ten new 'Shared Neighbourhood Developments'; and conducting a review of housing to bring forward recommendations on how to enhance shared neighbourhoods.[373]

In February 2016, the NI Housing Executive formally launched its 'Community Cohesion Strategy 2015-20' which is delivered across five themes including: segregation/integration; race relations; communities in transition; interface areas; flags, emblems and sectional symbols. In relation to residential segregation and integration, the strategy contains a number of actions including: supporting research into segregated and shared housing including updating the Mapping Segregation report; facilitating and encouraging mixed housing schemes in the social and affordable sector; and work with Office of the First Minister and the Deputy First Minister (now the Executive Office), the Department of Social Development (now the Department for Communities), Housing Associations and others to bring proposals forward for ten Shared Future capital build projects of mixed housing schemes in the medium term. The strategy also commits to developing programmes of action to address issues of residential segregation and integration across three years, as well as developing legacy programmes targeting young champions in neighbourhoods.[374]

The Equality Commission for NI assessed the 'Facing the Future: Housing Strategy for NI 2012-2017' and 'Building Successful Communities' from an equality perspective. It found that the former Department of Social Development (now Department for Communities) failed to comply with a number of its Equality Scheme commitments in relation to these strategies. The Equality Commission concluded that, with the 'Facing the Future: Housing Strategy for NI 2012 – 2017', the Department failed to meet its screening and equality impact assessment commitments in a timely manner. The Equality Commission also concluded that the Department failed to meet its Equality Scheme commitments in respect of screening and equality impact assessment when 'Building Successful Communities'' was launched, specifically with respect to the selection of pilot areas. As part of the Investigation, the Equality Commission also considered two other documents - the 'Housing Strategy Action Plan 2012-2017' and the 'Social Housing Reform Programme'. It concluded that the Department did meet the commitments relating to screening and equality impact assessment set out the relevant Equality Scheme in respect of these documents.[375]

The Commission recommended to the UN ICESCR Committee in 2016 that proactive concentrated efforts were taken to promote the development of shared social housing within a clear time-frame to improve community relations in NI.[376] The UN ICESCR Committee's concluding observations urged the UK to:

intensify its efforts to address the challenges to overcome persistent inequalities in housing for Catholic families in North Belfast, including through meaningful participation of all actors in decision-making processes related to housing.[377]

Data Collection

The Equality Commission for NI's assessment of the 'Facing the Future: Housing Strategy for NI 2012-2017' and 'Building Successful Communities' found that, despite monitoring guidance for public authorities, there is a lack of robust housing and communities data relating to a number equality grounds including: gender; gender identity; religion; race; political opinion; and sexual orientation.[378]

373   OFMDFM, Together: Building a United Community Strategy – (TBUC), 2013, pp. 27 and 54.

374   NIHE, Community Cohesion Strategy 2015-2020, 2015, p. 34.

375   ECNI, Investigation Report under Schedule 9 of the NI Act 1998: Department for Social Development - Housing Policy Proposals, November 2015.

376   NIHRC, Submission to the UN Committee on Economic, Social and Cultural Rights 58th Session on the Sixth Periodic Report of the United Kingdom's Compliance with ICESCR, April 2016, pp. 58-59.

377   UN Committee on Economic, Social and Cultural Rights, Concluding observations on the sixth periodic report of the United Kingdom of Great Britain and Northern Ireland E/C.12/GBR/CO/6, UN Economic and Social Council, 14 July 2016, para. 50(e).

378   ECNI, Investigation Report under Schedule 9 of the NI Act 1998: Department for Social Development - Housing Policy Proposals, November 2015.

The Commission's 2016 parallel report to the UN ICESCR Committee recommended that the UK collects robust equality data to assess and monitor inequalities in housing and to allow for evaluation of Government Department actions to address inequalities in NI.[379]

Homelessness

Statistics

In 2015/16, 18,628 households presented as homeless to the NI Housing Executive with 11,202 being accepted as full duty applicants.[380] There are concerns for the 'hidden homeless' – those whose applications were rejected (7,426 in 2015/16) and the unknown number of homeless who do not apply in the first place.

Homelessness arises due to a combination of factors. The primary reasons cited by the NI Housing Executive are, 'sharing breakdown/family dispute, accommodation not reasonable and loss of rented accommodation'.[381] Economic pressures, mental health and addiction can also have an impact.[382]

Research has shown that the rates for statutory homeless acceptances are higher in NI than anywhere elsewhere in the UK. In 2015/16, statutory acceptances per 1,000 households in NI ran at 14.8 per cent compared to 11.7 per cent in Scotland, in Wales, 3.6 per cent and 2.3 per cent in England.[383]

The 'Homelessness Strategy for NI 2012-2017' aims to eliminate long-term homelessness and rough sleeping across NI by 2020. The strategic objectives for achieving this include placing homelessness prevention at the forefront of service delivery; reducing the length of time households and individuals experience homelessness by improving access to affordable housing; removing the need to sleep rough; and improving services to vulnerable homeless households and individuals. The strategy also highlighted that an effective response to homelessness requires an integrated strategy that involves collaboration between the statutory, voluntary and community sectors.[384]

The Commission raised these issues with the UN ICESCR Committee in June 2016[385] and the Special Rapporteur on Adequate Housing in July 2016.[386] The UN ICESCR Committee in its 2016 concluding observations on the UK urged the UK:

> *to take immediate measures, including by allocating appropriate funds to local authorities, to reduce the exceptionally high levels of homelessness, particularly in England and NI, and to ensure adequate provision of reception facilities, including emergency shelters, hostels and reception, as well as social rehabilitation centres.*[387]

---

379 NIHRC, Submission to the UN Committee on Economic, Social and Cultural Rights 58th Session on the Sixth Periodic Report of the United Kingdom's Compliance with ICESCR, April 2016, pp. 57-58.

380 http://www.nihe.gov.uk/homelessness_information

381 http://www.nihe.gov.uk/homelessness_information

382 Patient and Client Council, Issues faced by People who are Homeless in Accessing Health and Social Care Services – Report of an Initial Scoping Exercise, HSCNI, 2015, p. 5; Suzanne Fitzpatrick et al, The Homelessness Monitor: Northern Ireland 2013, Crisis, 2013, p. ix.

383 Suzanne Fitzpatrick et al, The Homelessness Monitor: Northern Ireland 2016, Crisis, 2016, p. 52.

384 NIHE, Homelessness Strategy for NI 2012-2017; 2012, p. 17.

385 NIHRC, Submission to the UN Committee on Economic, Social and Cultural Rights 58th Session on the Sixth Periodic Report of the United Kingdom's Compliance with ICESCR, April 2016, pp. 49-50.

386 NIHRC, Submission to the Special Rapporteur on Adequate Housing Regarding the Link Between the Right to Life and the Right to Adequate Housing, 2016.

387 UN Committee on Economic, Social and Cultural Rights, Concluding observations on the sixth periodic report of the United Kingdom of Great Britain and Northern Ireland E/C.12/GBR/CO/6, UN Economic and Social Council, 14 July 2016, para 52.

The UN ICESCR Committee also urged the UK to:

take specific measures to deal with the inability of renters in the private rental sector to pay rents on account of the limits imposed on housing allowance and to effectively regulate the private rental sector, including through security of tenure protection and accountability mechanisms.[388]

Homelessness and Health

The average age of life-expectancy for homeless people sleeping rough or residing in shelters and homeless hostels is 43 years of age for women and 48 for men. This is on average 30 years lower than the average age of life-expectancy across the general population.[389] The NI Housing Executive estimates that less than ten individuals sleep rough in NI per night. If services were not available it is estimated that this figure would rise to 100 individuals.[390]

The NI Housing Executive's 'Housing and Health Strategy' examined the contribution of housing to health and recognised the need for partnership working with the health sector and also statutory, voluntary and community sectors. It also recognised a link between inadequate housing and health.

The Commission in its parallel report to the UN ICESCR Committee recommended that consideration should be given to incorporating the Housing Health and Safety Rating System into a reformed housing fitness standard for NI.[391] The Commission also reported the above findings to the UN Special Rapporteur on Adequate Housing in July 2016. The UN ICESCR Committee in its 2016 concluding observations urged the UK to 'take corrective measures to address bad housing or sub-standard housing conditions and inhabitability'.[392]

Complex Needs

A number of homeless persons died on the street in Belfast in early 2016.[393] The Social Development Committee of the NI Assembly was informed that some of these individuals were to varying degrees users of homelessness services.[394]

Significant investment has been given in recent years to the delivery of homelessness services. For example, in Belfast, there has been an investment of £13m to deliver homelessness services. It has been highlighted to the Social Development Committee of the NI Assembly that there are a small number of rough sleepers. The issue is much more than housing, as many of those who present as homeless have a range of complex needs, including mental health, addiction to alcohol or drugs, including psychoactive substances, dual diagnosis and personality disorder. Pathways into services can be complex, difficult to access and a person may have to reach a critical stage before any intervention is offered. Suggestions to tackle the issue made by practitioners working in organisations dealing with homelessness included: a need for housing solutions with wraparound support, detox facilities for homeless people, and delivery of specialist support at the point of contact.[395]

388 UN Committee on Economic, Social and Cultural Rights, Concluding observations on the sixth periodic report of the United Kingdom of Great Britain and Northern Ireland E/C.12/GBR/CO/6, UN Economic and Social Council, 14 July 2016, para 50(b).

389 Patient and Client Council, Issues faced by People who are Homeless in Accessing Health and Social Care Services – Report of an Initial Scoping Exercise, HSCNI, 2015, p. 5.

390 NIHE, Homelessness Strategy for NI 2012-2017, 2012, p. 22.

391 NIHRC, Submission to the UN Committee on Economic, Social and Cultural Rights 58th Session on the Sixth Periodic Report of the United Kingdom's Compliance with ICESCR, April 2016, pp. 51-52.

392 UN Committee on Economic, Social and Cultural Rights, Concluding observations on the sixth periodic report of the United Kingdom of Great Britain and Northern Ireland E/C.12/GBR/CO/6, UN Economic and Social Council, 14 July 2016, para 50(c).

393 BBC News NI, 'Belfast city centre: Homeless man found dead 'loveable rogue'', 8 February 2016. Available at: http://www.bbc.co.uk/news/uk-northern-ireland-35522393; Allan Preston, 'City homelessness summit after three deaths in fortnight', Belfast Telegraph, 19 February 2016. Available at: http://www.belfasttelegraph.co.uk/news/northern-ireland/city-homelessness-summit-after-three-deaths-in-fortnight-34466980.html; Angela Rainey, 'Homeless action call as fourth man dies in Belfast', Belfast Telegraph, 26 February 2016. Available at: http://www.belfasttelegraph.co.uk/news/northern-ireland/homeless-action-call-as-fourth-man-dies-in-belfast-34487459.html; BBC News NI, 'Belfast: Homeless woman dies in shop doorway', 19 March 2016. Available at: http://www.bbc.co.uk/news/uk-northern-ireland-35853752.

394 Committee for Social Development Meeting, 3 March 2016. Available at https://niassembly.tv/video/committee-social-development-meeting-03-march-2016/.

395 Committee for Social Development Meeting, 3 March 2016. Available at https://niassembly.tv/video/committee-social-development-meeting-03-march-2016/.

A Ministerial High-Level Group was established, comprising of the Ministers for Communities, Health and Justice in response to the developments. The Social Development Committee has called for a holistic approach to support the homeless and rough sleepers. The Social Development Committee welcomed the establishment of the Ministerial High Level Group and stated:

It is our sincere hope that this will provide a genuine opportunity to develop new proposals and practical action plans to enhance collaboration and co-ordination between the Departments and to ultimately deliver a better service to the homeless here.[396]

The Commission recommended to the UN ICESCR Committee that the UK Government should ensure there is an increased emphasis on a joint delivery of services to address homelessness in relation to persons with complex needs including physical and mental health issues as well as substance abuse in NI.[397] The Commission also raised these issues with the Special Rapporteur on Adequate Housing in July 2016.

The UN ICESCR Committee in its 2016 concluding observations on the UK urged the UK:

to adopt all necessary measures to avoid the criminalisation of "rough sleeping" in the State Party and to develop appropriate policies and programmes to facilitate the social reintegration of homeless persons. In this respect, the Committee draws the attention of the State Party to its General Comment No 4 (1991) on the right to adequate housing.[398]

Repossession and Mortgages

The Mortgage Repossession Taskforce was established by the former Department of Social Development (now the Department for Communities) in 2014 following concerns about higher levels of repossessions and negative equity in NI, compared to other parts of the UK.[399] The Taskforce reported in February 2015 that:

while affordability problems or the risk of repossession may be familiar to many households in Great Britain, the magnitude of the crash in NI fundamentally distinguishes the region from the aggregate UK picture. As a result of the heavier impact there is a bigger proportion of households with problem debt and at risk of repossession in NI than in other parts of the UK.

The Taskforce made recommendations including the development of a Mortgage Options Hub to support individuals and families facing repossession.[400] Officials from the former Department of Social Development (now Department for Communities) informed the Social Development Committee in February 2016 that significant progress has been made on a number of the recommendations. Funding for the Mortgage Debt Advice Service has been increased by 50 per cent to £340,000 a year. The Minister for Justice agreed to fund the Court Duty Possession Scheme provided by the Housing Rights Service until 2018.

The Commission recommended to the UN ICESCR Committee in 2016 that the UK took account of the Mortgage Repossession Taskforce's recommendations and considered introducing a Mortgage Rescue Scheme in NI.[401]

---

396 Committee for Social Development Meeting, 3 March 2016. Available at https://niassembly.tv/video/committee-social-development-meeting-03-march-2016/.

397 NIHRC, Submission to the UN Committee on Economic, Social and Cultural Rights 58th Session on the Sixth Periodic Report of the United Kingdom's Compliance with ICESCR, April 2016, pp. 52-53.

398 UN Committee on Economic, Social and Cultural Rights, Concluding observations on the sixth periodic report of the United Kingdom of Great Britain and Northern Ireland E/C.12/GBR/CO/6, UN Economic and Social Council, 14 July 2016, para. 52.

399 See Housing Rights Website.

400 DSD, Housing Repossession Taskforce: Final Report, February 2015.

401 NIHRC, Submission to the UN Committee on Economic, Social and Cultural Rights 58th Session on the Sixth Periodic Report of the United Kingdom's Compliance with ICESCR, April 2016, pp. 55-57.

The waiting time for the financial support for new claimants on certain means tested benefits, the Support for Mortgage Interest, was reduced to 13 weeks in January 2009 as a response to the recession. In April 2016 the waiting time was reinstated as 39 weeks.[402]

The Commission reported to the UN ICESCR Committee in 2016 that there are a higher proportion of people in debt and at risk of repossession in NI compared to the rest of the UK and that the most common reason for repossessions in NI is arrears in mortgage repayments. The Commission recommended to the UN ICESCR Committee that the UK consider what actions to take to mitigate the impact of increasing the Support for Mortgage Interest waiting times in NI and how to monitor the impact of the changes.[403]

Travellers accommodation

Supply

Within the UK, including NI, there is a 'shortage of adequate stopping sites for Roma/Gypsies and Irish Travellers'.[404] The NI Housing Executive reported in 2014 that, within NI, there was a gross need for 18 units of grouped accommodation, 28 serviced site pitches, two transit site pitches, 51 units of social housing and 13 units of other accommodation forms.[405] Since 2011 the NI Housing Executive had made four planning applications for Travellers' accommodation, with three accepted. One application relating to the Rathenraw site was appealed. The appeal is ongoing.[406]

In 2011, the Advisory Committee on the FCNM urged the UK authorities:

to ensure that planning permission for caravan sites is granted in a way that duly takes into account the specific needs of Gypsies and Travellers and results in an increase in the availability of sites.[407]

The Commission, in its 2016 parallel report, advised the UN ICESCR Committee to recommend that the UK ensure planning rules take into account the needs of Travellers in NI.[408] The UN ICESCR Committee in its 2016 Concluding Observations urged the UK to:

ensure adequate access to culturally appropriate accommodation and stopping sites for the Roma, Gypsy and Traveller communities, as appropriate, take steps to avoid all discrimination in the provision of accommodation.[409]

Site Licences

There is a legislative anomaly that requires the NI Housing Executive to obtain site licences from local councils, which 'can create practical difficulties in ensuring adequate site provision'.[410] The former Department of Social Development (now Department for Communities) in March 2016 reported that

---

402   https://www.nidirect.gov.uk/articles/getting-help-make-your-mortgage-interest-payments

403   NIHRC, Submission to the UN Committee on Economic, Social and Cultural Rights 58th Session on the Sixth Periodic Report of the United Kingdom's Compliance with ICESCR, April 2016, pp. 55-56.

404   UN Committee on Economic, Social and Cultural Rights, Concluding observations on the sixth periodic report of the United Kingdom of Great Britain and Northern Ireland E/C.12/GBR/CO/6, UN Economic and Social Council, 14 July 2016, para 30.

405   NIHE, Traveller Accommodation Needs Assessment 2014, 2014, p. 29.

406   Information obtained from DSD (March 2016).

407   Advisory Committee on the Framework Convention for the Protection of National Minorities, Third Opinion on the United Kingdom adopted on 30 June 2011 ACFC/OP/III(2011)006, 22 December 2011, para 98.

408   NIHRC, Submission to the UN Committee on Economic, Social and Cultural Rights 58th Session on the Sixth Periodic Report of the United Kingdom's Compliance with ICESCR, April 2016, pp. 59-60.

409   UN Committee on Economic, Social and Cultural Rights, Concluding observations on the sixth periodic report of the United Kingdom of Great Britain and Northern Ireland E/C.12/GBR/CO/6, UN Economic and Social Council, 14 July 2016, para 50(d).

410   NIHRC, Submission to the UN Committee on Economic, Social and Cultural Rights 58th Session on the Sixth Periodic Report of the United Kingdom's Compliance with ICESCR, April 2016, p. 59.

there was one pending site licence application before Craigavon Borough Council and at that time the application had not been granted.[411]

In 2011, the Advisory Committee on the FCNM expressed concern that the NI Housing Executive had not met its objectives in providing additional sites for Travellers, and identified that the need for the NI Housing Executive to obtain licences from local councils in order to deliver new sites seemed to be one of the reasons for a lack of delivery.[412]

The Commission, in its 2016 parallel report, advised the UN ICESCR Committee to recommend that the UK address the legislative anomaly and remove the need to obtain site licences from District Councils in NI.[413]

Statistics

The official figures for the Traveller population in NI do not appear to reflect reality making it difficult to create and evaluate appropriate polices and strategies. The NI Housing Executive has recorded that between 2002 and 2014, the Traveller community population in NI fluctuated between 1,220 and 1,480.[414] The NI Government Partnership on Travellers' issues estimated that a more accurate approximation would be a Traveller population of between 3,500 and 4,000 persons.[415]

In 2011, the Advisory Committee of the FCNM urged the UK authorities to improve the coordination of the different levels of authorities involved in sites delivery and pursuing regular monitoring of the accommodation needs of Gypsies and Travellers.[416]

Adequacy

Research suggests that the overall standard of Travellers' accommodation is inadequate. A quarter of Traveller respondents residing in NI considered their place of residence to be unhealthy or very unhealthy, with 29 per cent describing their residence as unsafe.[417] A lack of footpaths, public lighting, fire hydrants, safe play areas, plumbing, washing facilities, electricity and refuse management has been reported.[418]

In 2011, the Advisory Committee of the FCNM urged the UK authorities at national and regional level 'to take far more vigorous measures to meet the accommodation needs of Gypsies and Travellers'. This includes:

developing further gender-sensitive and comprehensive strategies, in close consultation with Gypsies and Travellers, in particular women belonging to these communities that duly take into account their other needs.[419]

All of these findings are due to be updated following the Advisory Committee's country visit to the UK in March 2016.

---

411   Information obtained from DSD (March 2016).

412   Advisory Committee on the Framework Convention for the Protection of National Minorities: Third Opinion on the United Kingdom for the Protection of National Minorities, ACFC/OP/III (2011)006, Council of Europe, para 94.

413   NIHRC, Submission to the UN Committee on Economic, Social and Cultural Rights 58th Session on the Sixth Periodic Report of the United Kingdom's Compliance with ICESCR, April 2016, pp. 59-61.

414   NIHE, Traveller Accommodation Needs Assessment 2002, p. 10; NIHE, Traveller Accommodation Needs Assessment 2008, p. 10; NIHE, Traveller Accommodation Needs Assessment 2014, p. 9.

415   Minutes of the 429th Meeting of the NI Housing Council, Armagh City Hotel, 14 April 2016, p. 3.

416   Advisory Committee on the Framework Convention for the Protection of National Minorities, Third Opinion on the United Kingdom adopted on 30 June 2011 ACFC/OP/III(2011)006, 22 December 2011, para 95.

417   ECNI, Outlining Minimum Standards for Traveller Accommodation, 2009, pp. 9-10.

418   Safa Abdella et al, Our Geels: All Ireland Traveller Health Study, UCD, 2010, p. 46; NICEM, The Annual Human Rights and Racial Equality Benchmarking Report 2013/14, OFMDFM, 2014, p. 96.

419   Advisory Committee on the Framework Convention for the Protection of National Minorities, Third Opinion on the United Kingdom adopted on 30 June 2011 ACFC/OP/III(2011)006, 22 December 2011, para 95.

The Commission, in its 2016 parallel report, advised the UN ICESCR Committee to recommend that the UK complies with the Housing (NI) Order 2003 to improve basic living conditions on serviced and halting sites in NI.[420] The UN ICESCR Committee in its 2016 concluding observations on the UK expressed concern that:

> *Travellers continue to face barriers in accessing adequate and culturally appropriate accommodation across [the UK], with adequate access to basic services, such as water and sanitation.*[421]

Commission's Investigation

On 1 September 2016 the Commission launched an investigation into Travellers' accommodation in NI. The investigation exercises the Commission's powers under Section 69 of the NI Act 1998. The Investigation focuses on providing a human rights analysis of good practices and issues that arise in relation to the right to adequate housing, in the context of Travellers' accommodation. It involves gathering and analysing evidence from the relevant public authorities, civil society organisations and members of the Traveller communities in NI. The findings of the Investigation will be published in autumn 2017.[422]

Unauthorised encampments (NI) Order 2005

The powers under the Unauthorised Encampments (NI) Order 2005 are rarely used. The former Department of Social Development (now Department for Communities) has reviewed the 2005 Order on an annual basis since it was commenced. Figures obtained from the former Department of Social Development in October 2015 showed that over the previous two years there was a noticeable decrease in police involvement in relation to unauthorised encampments. One direction was issued during that monitoring period and on only two occasions over a seven-year period was a vehicle confiscated.[423] A roundtable discussion held by the Commission with non-governmental organisations that work with Travellers in September 2016 led to feedback that the threat of using the legislation is often sufficient to have an impact.[424]

The Commission advised the UN ICESCR Committee to re-recommend that the UK repeal the provisions of the Unauthorised Encampments (NI) Order 2005 in NI.[425] The UN ICESCR Committee has consistently expressed concern at how the Unauthorised Encampments (NI) Order 2005 'makes Roma/Gypsies and Irish Travellers liable to be evicted from their homes, to have their homes destroyed and then to be imprisoned and/or fined'.[426] The UN ICESCR Committee has consistently called for this legislation to be repealed.

The NI Housing Executive operates a co-operation policy. This policy permits Travellers to set up an unauthorised encampment on public land for which there is no current or immediate use and permits them to occupy the land provided it does not create a public health or traffic hazard and the land is

420 NIHRC, Submission to the UN Committee on Economic, Social and Cultural Rights 58th Session on the Sixth Periodic Report of the United Kingdom's Compliance with ICESCR, April 2016, pp. 59-62.

421 UN Committee on Economic, Social and Cultural Rights, Concluding Observations of the CESCR: United Kingdom of Great Britain and NI, the Crown Dependencies and the Overseas Dependent Territories, E/C.12/GBR/CO/5, UN Economic and Social Council, 22 May 2009, para 30; UN Committee on Economic, Social and Cultural Rights, Concluding observations on the sixth periodic report of the United Kingdom of Great Britain and Northern Ireland E/C.12/GBR/CO/6, UN Economic and Social Council, 14 July 2016, para 49.

422 NIHRC, Travellers' Accommodation Investigation Terms of Reference, September 2016.

423 Information obtained from the DSD, October 2015.

424 Roundtable discussion on Travellers' accommodation in NI held with non-governmental organisations working with Travellers, 20 September 2016.

425 NIHRC, Submission to the UN Committee on Economic, Social and Cultural Rights 58th Session on the Sixth Periodic Report of the United Kingdom's Compliance with ICESCR, April 2016, pp. 61-62.

426 UN Committee on Economic, Social and Cultural Rights, Concluding Observations of the CESCR: United Kingdom of Great Britain and NI, the Crown Dependencies and the Overseas Dependent Territories, E/C.12/GBR/CO/5, UN Economic and Social Council, 22 May 2009, para 30; UN Committee on Economic, Social and Cultural Rights, Concluding observations on the sixth periodic report of the United Kingdom of Great Britain and Northern Ireland E/C.12/GBR/CO/6, UN Economic and Social Council, 14 July 2016, para 49.

maintained in a reasonable and orderly manner.[427] The NI Housing Executive emphasises that the policy is not a substitute for permanent or transit sites but is intended to act as a way of dealing with a humane requirement.[428]

In its 2016 Parallel Reports to the Advisory Committee on the FCNM[429] and the UN ICESCR Committee,[430] the Commission welcomed the co-operation policy, but advised that the measures in the 2005 Order potentially have a chilling impact; these measures enable a national minority to become liable to criminal prosecution for following their traditional lifestyle in a context of inadequate site provision.

Anti-poverty strategy

In June 2015 the NI High Court ruled that the NI Executive had failed to adopt an identifiable strategy setting out how it proposes to tackle poverty, social exclusion and patterns of deprivation based on objective need in furtherance of its obligation to do so under the NI Act 1998 section 28E. Mr. Justice Treacy ruled:

> *The Oxford English Dictionary defines a "strategy" as a "plan of action designed to achieve a long term or overall aim". In adopting only the "architecture and principles", the Executive adopted something that was inchoate. There is no evidence before me that this inchoate strategy was ever finalised. There is no evidence that it was ever crafted into a road map designed to tackle the issues referred to in the section.*[431]

The NI Poverty Bulletin for 2014/15 reports that 22 per cent of individuals were in poverty (395,100), compared to 21 per cent the previous year. The figures showed that 21 per cent of working age adults were in poverty (226,400), compared to 20 per cent the previous year. In relation to children living in poverty in 2014/15, the bulletin highlighted that 25 per cent of children were in poverty (109,500) compared to 23 per cent the previous year. The figures for pensioners living in poverty in 2014/15 estimated at one percentage point lower at 20 per cent (59,200) than in 2013/14 at 21 per cent.[432]

The Joseph Rowntree Foundation highlighted in its 2016 report that NI has not enjoyed the same strong employment performance as Great Britain, noting that since 2011, the working age employment rate has increased by 0.6 per cent, compared with a 3.0 per cent increase in Great Britain. The report noted that thinking around poverty in NI is dominated by one short term development (the Welfare Reform Mitigations Package) and one longer term development (the Executive must now develop an anti-poverty strategy). The Joseph Rowntree Foundation concluded that the strategy needs to face up to the potential problems caused by welfare reform as well as the changing composition of the poverty landscape, where there are more young people, private renters and working families in low income.[433]

The Commission informed the UN ICESCR Committee in April 2016 that an Anti- Poverty Strategy based on objective need remains outstanding, despite the High Court ruling in 2015.[434] The UN ICESCR Committee in its 2016 concluding observations expressed its concern about the disproportionate, adverse impact that austerity measures introduced in 2010 are having on the enjoyment of economic,

427   DSD, Guide to the Unauthorised Encampments (NI) Order 2005, 2006.

428   NIHE, 'Our Cooperation Policy for Travellers'. Available at: http://www.nihe.gov.uk/index/advice/advice_for_travellers/co-operation_policy.htm

429   NIHRC, Submission to the Advisory Committee on the Framework Convention for the Protection of National Minorities: Parallel Report to the Advisory Committee on the Fourth Monitoring Report of the UK, 2016, p. 104.

430   NIHRC, Submission to the UN Committee on Economic, Social and Cultural Rights 58th Session on the Sixth Periodic Report of the United Kingdom's Compliance with ICESCR, April 2016, pp. 59-62.

431   NICTS Press Release, 'Court Finds Executive Failed to Adopt Strategy on Poverty and social Exclusion: Summary of Judgment', 30th June 2015.

432   NISRA, Northern Ireland Poverty Bulletin, 28 June 2016, p. 1.

433   Joseph Rowntree Foundation, Monitoring Social Exclusion in Northern Ireland, March 2016.

434   NIHRC, Submission to the UN Committee on Economic, Social and Cultural Rights on the 6th Periodic Report of the UK's compliance with ICESCR, April 2016, paras 26.1-26.5.

social and cultural rights by disadvantaged and marginalized individuals and groups. The Committee also recommended that the State party take steps to introduce measures to guarantee targeted support to all those living in poverty or at risk of poverty, in particular persons with disabilities, persons belonging to ethnic, religious or other minorities, single-parent families and families with children, and adopt an anti-poverty strategy in NI.[435]

The Draft Programme for Government Outcomes Framework refers to poverty reduction as one of its indicators.[436] The Commission advised the NI Executive that an anti-poverty strategy based on objective need remains outstanding and that the issue should be addressed as a matter of priority.[437] According to an Assembly question, the strategy is expected to be published for consultation in 2016.[438]

The Minister for Communities was asked in an Assembly question when formulating his Department's anti-poverty strategy, whether he will take account of the United Nations High Commissioner for Human Rights' report entitled Principles and Guidelines for a Human Rights Approach to Poverty Reduction Strategies. The Minister responded:

I am aware of the Report the member refers to and, indeed, agree with the UN High Commissioner for Human Rights when she says that 'yet another feature of the Human Rights approach is that poverty reduction becomes a shared responsibility.' The definition of 'overall poverty' adopted by the UN includes social discrimination and exclusion. This is precisely why we have incorporated our work to tackle poverty in a much wider social strategy looking at all these inter-related issues. Our draft Social Strategy will recognise that measuring poverty on the basis of income alone will not show the full picture. The human rights approach set out in the Report 'underlines the multidimensional nature of poverty, describing poverty in terms of a range of interrelated and mutually reinforcing deprivations, and drawing attention to the stigma, discrimination, insecurity and social exclusion associated with poverty'. The draft Executive Social Strategy will seek to promote opportunity for everyone and tackle poverty and social exclusion.[439]

🟠 Child poverty strategy

The Welfare Reform and Work Act 2016, which received royal assent in March 2016, repealed the duty to meet time-bound targets on child poverty as originally set out in the Child Poverty Act 2010. These targets have been replaced by a statutory duty to publish an annual report on the extent and educational attainment of children in poverty. These changes extend to NI.

The 'NI Child Poverty Strategy'[440] and 'Child Poverty Strategy Annual Report for 2014/2015'[441] were both published in March 2016. The strategy adopts an outcomes based approach. The strategy sets out the indicators that will be used to measure its achievements, including two headline indicators, which are two of the measures set out in the Child Poverty Act 2010, absolute child poverty and relative child poverty. The NI Executive states that 'the strategy and its action plan deals with the current situation and will be reviewed and revised, as necessary, on an ongoing basis'.

---

435   UN Committee on Economic, Social and Cultural Rights, Concluding observations on the sixth periodic report of the United Kingdom of Great Britain and Northern Ireland E/C.12/GBR/CO/6, UN Economic and Social Council, 14 July 2016, para 48.

436   Northern Ireland Executive, Draft Programme for Government Framework 2016-21, p. 13.

437   NIHRC, Human Rights Priorities for the 2016 Programme for Government,July 2016, p. 14.

438   AQW 2283/16-21, Ms Michelle Gildernew.

439   AQO 431/16-21, Mr Declan McAleer.

440   NI Executive, The Executive's Child Poverty Strategy, March 2016.

441   NI Executive, Annual Report on Child Poverty 2014-2015, March 2016.

In 2016, the Commission recommended that the eradication of child poverty in NI was analysed against the (now former) targets set by the UK Government to eliminate Child Poverty by 2020.[442] The UN ICESCR Committee subsequently expressed concern that the UK:

does not have a specific definition of poverty and that the new Life Chances Strategy, as contained in the Welfare Reform and Work Act 2016, has repealed the duty to meet time-bound targets on child poverty, which remains high and is projected to increase in the future, especially in NI (art. 11).[443]

The UN ICESCR Committee urged the UK to develop a comprehensive child poverty strategy and to reinstate the targets and reporting duties on child poverty.[444]

The UN CRC Committee also reviewed UK's performance in 2016. The UN CRC Committee noted that 'the rate of child poverty remains high...and affects children in Wales and NI the most'.[445]

The UK was urged by the UN CRC Committee to:

(a) Set up clear accountability mechanisms for the eradication of child poverty, including by re-establishing concrete targets with a set time frame and measurable indicators, and continue regular monitoring and reporting on child poverty reduction in all parts of the State party;

(b) Ensure clear focus on the child in the State party's poverty reduction strategies and action plans, including in the new "Life Chances Strategy", and support the production and implementation of child poverty reduction strategies in the devolved administrations;

(c) Conduct a comprehensive assessment of the cumulative impact of the full range of social security and tax credit reforms introduced between 2010 and 2016 on children, including children with disabilities and children belonging to ethnic minority groups;

(d) Where necessary, revise the mentioned reforms in order to fully respect the right of the child to have his or her best interests taken as a primary consideration, taking into account the different impacts of the reform on different groups of children, particularly those in vulnerable situations.[446]

Reduction in asylum financial support

People who claim asylum are not permitted to work while they are awaiting the processing of their claim. However, claimants can access asylum support under section 95 of the Immigration and Asylum Act 1999. On 16 July 2015, new Regulations came into force introducing a flat rate in asylum support to take effect from 10 August 2015. The standard rate is now £36.95 per week provided to each supported person of all ages.[447] This cash amount is in addition to free accommodation and free medical care; dental care and free education for children from age five to age 17.[448]

The Refugee Council called on the UK Government to commission an independent review into the adequacy of current support levels before implementing the reductions.[449]

---

442 NIHRC, Submission to the UN Committee on Economic, Social and Cultural Rights 58th Session on the Sixth Periodic Report of the United Kingdom's Compliance with ICESCR, April 2016, p. 44.

443 UN Committee on the Rights of the Child, Concluding Observations on the Sixth Periodic Report of the United Kingdom of Great Britain and NI, E/C.12/GBR/CO/6, UN CRC, 24 June 2016, para 48.

444 UN Committee on the Rights of the Child, Concluding Observations on the Sixth Periodic Report of the United Kingdom of Great Britain and NI, E/C.12/GBR/CO/6, UN CRC, 24 June 2016, para 48.

445 UN Committee on the Rights of the Child, Concluding Observations on the Sixth Periodic Report of the United Kingdom of Great Britain and NI, E/C.12/GBR/CO/6, UN CRC, 24 June 2016, para 70(a).

446 UN Committee on the Rights of the Child, Concluding Observations on the Sixth Periodic Report of the United Kingdom of Great Britain and NI, E/C.12/GBR/CO/6, UN CRC, 24 June 2016, paras 71(a)-71(d).

447 Regulation 2 of The Asylum Support (Amendment No.3) Regulations 2015.

448 Explanatory Memorandum to The Asylum Support (Amendment No.3) Regulations 2015.

449 Refugee Council, ''Families' asylum support drastically cut', 16 July 2015.

The House of Lords debated a motion to annul the Regulations in October 2015, however, the motion was not agreed. A further motion to regret the Regulations was not moved.[450]

In August 2015 the Home Office consulted on proposals to reform existing support to failed asylum seeker and other "illegal migrants". The proposals included:[451]

- *Repealing section 4(1) of the Immigration and Asylum Act, which provides support to those on temporary admission, and those temporarily or otherwise released from immigration detention. Section 95 support will be available for those who are destitute;*

- *Closing off section 4(2) support for failed asylum seekers who make no effort to leave the UK at the point that their asylum claim is rejected. Support would continue to be available to those whose claim had finally been rejected but could not be expected to avoid destitution by leaving the UK because they had lodged further submissions with the Home Office that were outstanding;*

- *Change section 95 support arrangements so that those who have a dependent child or children with them when their asylum claim is refused and any appeal is finally rejected are no longer classed as "asylum seekers" for the purposes of eligibility for support;*

- *Placing the onus on those who have failed an asylum application to apply for support before a 28 day grace period demonstrating why they are unable to leave the UK and why they face destitution.*

In response to the consultation, the Commission advised the Home Office that the proposals are retrogressive concerning the enjoyment of the right to an adequate standard of living and the right to social security.[452] The Commission advised that given the strong presumption against retrogression, a full justification by reference to the totality of the rights provided for in the ICESCR and in the context of the full use of the maximum available resources should be given.

The Commission further advised that placing the onus on those with child dependents who have failed an asylum application to apply for support before a 28 day grace period demonstrating why they are unable to leave the UK and why they face destitution, is contrary to the best interests of the child principle. Furthermore, the Commission advised that the proposed safeguards to extend the grace period after 28 days and the possibility of an extension, on application, if there is a practical obstacle preventing the family's departure from the UK may not be sufficient to meet human rights requirements where asylum seekers and irregular migrants fall into destitution.[453]

In November 2015 the Home Office issued a response to the consultation, the Home Office indicated that in light of the responses received it would reflect on the length of the grace period.[454] The proposals remained unchanged and formed part of the Immigration Act 2016 which received royal assent in 2016.

The Commission raised its concerns regarding reductions in financial support for asylum seekers with the UN ICESCR Committee in its Parallel report in April 2016.[455] In June 2016 the UN ICESCR Committee expressed concern about the challenges faced by asylum seekers in the enjoyment of economic, social and cultural rights, particularly those that are due to restrictions in accessing

450 House of Lords Hansard of Debate on 27 October 2015.

451 Home Office, 'Reforming support for failed asylum seekers and other illegal migrants' consultation, August 2015, para 20.

452 NIHRC, Correspondence to Mr James Brokenshire MP Minister of State (Minister for Immigration), 8 September 2015.

453 NIHRC, 'Response to Home Office Consultation on Reforming Support for Failed Asylum Seekers and other illegal Migrants', September 2015.

454 Home Office, 'Reforming Support for Failed Asylum Seekers and Other Illegal Migrants : Response to Consultation', November 2015, para 2.4.3.

455 NIHRC, Submission to the UN Committee on Economic, Social and Cultural Rights on the 6th Periodic Report of the UK's compliance with ICESCR, April 2016, paras 29.1-29.4.

employment and the insufficient level of support provided through the daily allowance (art. 2 (2) and (11)).

The UN ICESCR Committee recommended that the State party:

increase the level of support provided to asylum seekers, including through the daily allowance, in order to ensure that they enjoy their economic, social and cultural rights, in particular the right to an adequate standard of living...[and] encourages the State party to ensure that asylum seekers are not restricted from accessing employment while their claims are being processed.[456]

In its 2016 report, the European Commission against Racism and Intolerance also recommended that:

taking steps to ensure that refugees do not fall into destitution by prolonging the provision of asylum support until access to welfare benefits is obtained.[457]

Crisis fund

In February and March 2015 the British Red Cross administered a Crisis Fund resourced by the former Office of the First Minister and Deputy First Minister (now the Executive Office).[458] The Crisis Fund was intended: 'to help minority ethnic individuals with no other means of support through emergency situations, such as vulnerable migrants, refugees and asylum seekers and other vulnerable groups'.[459]

In the two months that the fund was administered in 2015, there were 980 interventions and the fund directly assisted 440 individuals, who between them had 480 dependents. The majority (60 per cent) were aged between 21-40.[460] The main reasons for accessing the fund were problems with benefit entitlements (25 per cent), domestic violence (14 per cent) and issues around seeking employment (14 per cent).[461]

The Commission raised the issue of the Crisis Fund with the UN ICESCR Committee in its Parallel submission in April 2016, suggesting that the Committee recommend:

that the UK Government and NI Executive address the causes of destitution in the first instance, rather than rely on a discretionary fund to address destitution when it emerges.[462]

Whilst not explicitly referring to the Crisis Fund, the UN ICESCR Committee called on the UK to introduce measures to guarantee targeted support to all those living in poverty or at risk of poverty, including persons belonging to ethnic, religious or other minorities.[463]

The Crisis Fund became active again in September 2016 and will run until March 2017.

456 UN Committee on Economic, Social and Cultural Rights, Concluding observations on the sixth periodic report of the United Kingdom of Great Britain and Northern Ireland E/C.12/GBR/CO/6, UN Economic and Social Council, 14 July 2016, para 25.

457 European Commission against Racism and Intolerance, Report on the United Kingdom (fifth monitoring cycle), CRI(2016)38, Adopted on 29 June 2016, European Commission against Racism and Intolerance, 4 October 2016, para 114.

458 AQW 40200/11-15, Ms Anna Lo.

459 NI Executive, 'Junior Ministers Jennifer McCann and Jonathan Bell today outlined the benefits of the new Crisis Fund for vulnerable minority ethnic people,' 4 February 2015.

460 Scope NI, 'Crisis Fund: can a little go a very long way', 31 July 2015.

461 Scope NI, 'Crisis Fund: can a little go a long way?', 31 July 2015.

462 NIHRC, Submission to the UN Committee on Economic, Social and Cultural Rights 58th Session on the Sixth Periodic Report of the United Kingdom's Compliance with ICESCR, April 2016, paras 30.1-30.3.

463 UN Committee on Economic, Social and Cultural Rights, Concluding observations on the sixth periodic report of the United Kingdom of Great Britain and Northern Ireland E/C.12/GBR/CO/6, UN Economic and Social Council, 14 July 2016, para 48.

Carers

In November 2014 the Commission published a report into the human rights of carers, the report measures the recorded experiences of carers set against the international human rights obligations of the NI Executive and other relevant public authorities.[464] The report specifically focused on the experiences of younger carers and older carers. The Commission made fifteen targeted recommendations relating to the rights of carers directed to the Departments of the NI Executive. This included a review of the Carers Strategy which is now ten years old. The Department of Health has given no indication of its willingness to consider such a review.

During Carers Week in June 2016 the Commission launched a short film highlighting the human rights of carers.[465]

Supported lodgings for young adults

The former Department of Health, Social Services and Public Safety (now Department of Health) consulted in 2015 on draft Standards for Supported Lodgings for Young Adults setting out standards for supported lodgings service providers to ensure the provision of high quality social care and housing support.[466] The Commission provided advice to the Department on the Standards.[467]

The Commission welcomed the positive reference to the UN CRC included within the draft Standards.[468] However, the Commission also recommended that further references to the UN CRC, including an explicit reference to the general principles of the treaty, be included within the draft Standards. The Commission advised that the absence of any references to young persons with disabilities within the draft Standards was unacceptable.[469] In addition, the Commission advised that it is of critical importance that a young person in Supported Lodgings continues to fall within the ambit of the Children (NI) Order 1995, with full access to the range of services and entitlements afforded to an individual defined as a 'child in need' for this purpose.[470] The Commission noted that private entities may be commissioned to provide supported lodgings in NI, the Commission recommended that the finalised Standards should clearly state that service providers will deliver services in a manner that is fully compliant with domestic and international human rights standards.[471]

Following the consultation, the 'Minimum Standards for Support Lodgings for Young People and Young Adults Aged 16-21 in NI' were launched by then Health Minister, Simon Hamilton, in March 2016.[472] It specifies that the underpinning values of the Standards are the Children (NI) Order 1995, the UN CRC, the UN CRPD and the NI Executive's 'Ten Year Strategy for Children and Young People: Our Children, Our Pledge'. This reflected the Commission's recommendations. The final document does not include an explicit reference to the general principles of the UN CRC. The Standards do however specify that all service providers act in a manner that is fully compliant with domestic and international human rights standards, as per the Commission's recommendation.

---

464 NIHRC, 'The Human Rights of Carers in Northern Ireland', November 2015.

465 NIHRC, Film on Carer's Rights, 8 June 2016.

466 DHSSPS, 'Consultation on draft Standards for Supported Lodgings for Young Adults', 2015.

467 NIHRC, 'The Department of Health, Social Services and Public Safety consultation on the Draft Standards for Supported Lodgings for Young Adults (aged 16-21) in Northern Ireland', 2015.

468 NIHRC, 'The Department of Health, Social Services and Public Safety consultation on the Draft Standards for Supported Lodgings for Young Adults (aged 16-21) in Northern Ireland', 2015, para 10.

469 NIHRC, 'The Department of Health, Social Services and Public Safety consultation on the Draft Standards for Supported Lodgings for Young Adults (aged 16-21) in Northern Ireland', 2015, para 31.

470 NIHRC, 'The Department of Health, Social Services and Public Safety consultation on the Draft Standards for Supported Lodgings for Young Adults (aged 16-21) in Northern Ireland', 2015, para 44.

471 NIHRC, 'The Department of Health, Social Services and Public Safety consultation on the Draft Standards for Supported Lodgings for Young Adults (aged 16-21) in Northern Ireland', 2015, para 11.

472 Department of Health, 'Minimum standards for supported lodgings for young people and young adults (aged 16-21) in Northern Ireland', March 2016.

Right to health

ICESCR	Article 12
UNCRPD	Article 25
ESC	Article 11
CFREU	Article 35

Emergency healthcare

In 2015 the Commission published its report into emergency health care in NI.[473] The inquiry report included over 100 key findings. On publication of the report the Chief Commissioner stated:

The Commission considered quality, accountability and governance of the service. We visited emergency departments throughout NI during the day and night. We heard from dedicated staff striving to maintain patient dignity in an often challenging and crowded environment. In such circumstances there were reported instances where patients did not receive assistance with personal care needs, no pain relief, and no access to food and fluids. Of particular concern were cases involving end of life care, the inappropriate transfer of older patients from nursing homes and the experiences of those presenting to Accident & Emergency in mental health crisis, with dementia or disabilities.

The Commission made 26 recommendations including a recommendation that the Department of Health, Social Service and Public Safety (now the Department of Health) develop dedicated Emergency Department minimum care standards, rooted in human rights and providing a benchmark for patient experience within Emergency Departments. The standards should include criterion on, inter alia:

- *The promotion of dignity in Emergency Departments;*

- *Participation by individuals, their family members and other carers in the care provided in the Emergency Department setting;*

- *Measures covering staff behaviour and attitude, adequate facilities;*

- *Accessible mechanisms to provide feedback of Emergency Department experiences including complaints;*

- *The policies and procedures each Emergency Department should have including a hospital wide escalation policy to address overcrowding; and,*

- *Ways of helping to guarantee equality of access for particular groups of patients including older people, patients with dementia, rare diseases, sensory impairments and those presenting in mental health crisis.*[474]

473 NIHRC, 'Human Rights Inquiry: Emergency Health Care', May 2015.
474 NIHRC, 'Human Rights Inquiry: Emergency Health Care', May 2015, Recommendations.

In November 2015 the former Minister for Health, Social Services and Public Safety, Simon Hamilton, set out significant changes to the health and social care system in NI, stating:

We have too many layers in our system. I want to see the Department take firmer, strategic control of our Health and Social Care system with our Trusts responsible for the planning of care in their areas and the operational independence to deliver it. [475]

A consultation was conducted by the former Minister with a report published in March 2016. [476] The recommendations made in the report were aimed at reducing bureaucracy and increasing accountability. One step planned by the former Minister was to abolish the Health and Social Care Board. [477] The new Minister of Health, Michelle O'Neill, has publicly confirmed her commitment to continuing 'to drive reform of the health and social care services'. [478] In October 2016 the Minister of Health published a ten year vision for the transform of the health and social care system, entitled 'Health and Wellbeing 2026: Delivering Together'. Speaking at the launch of the vision the Minister stated:

Whole system transformation will take time and it will only be truly sustainable if there is meaningful engagement with clinicians, staff and patients to build a collective way forward. I believe by working in partnership with those who use and those who deliver services we can co-design, co-produce and implement the changes our population deserves. [479]

The Commission is tracking the progress of the Inquiry recommendations and is working with the Belfast Health and Social Care Trust and Northern Health and Social Care Trust to develop two pilot projects. The first is focus upon a human rights based approach to accident and emergency care. The second will deliver a participatory model of decision making on the future of community services.

⬤ Termination of pregnancy

On 11 December 2014 the Commission issued judicial review proceedings against the Department of Justice maintaining that the law on termination of pregnancy in NI violates the rights of women and girls by criminalising them when they seek a termination of pregnancy in circumstances of fatal and serious foetal abnormality, rape or incest. The Commission has repeatedly advised the Department of Justice that the existing law is, in the Commission's view, a violation of human rights.

The case was heard by the Honourable Mr Justice Horner on 15, 16 and 17 June 2015. The Attorney General for NI among others intervened in the case.

Speaking at the commencement of the case the Chief Commissioner stated:

It is appropriate for the Human Rights Commission to take this legal challenge in our own name. We recognise the particular sensitivities of the issue. It is a matter of significant public interest to ensure that the rights of vulnerable women and girls in these situations are protected. It is in everyone's interest that the law is clarified in this area. [480]

Justice Horner ruled on the 30 November 2015 that the law in NI breached the ECHR, Article 8 the right to private life and a women's right to personal autonomy by the absence of exceptions to the general prohibition on abortions in the cases of: (a) fatal foetal abnormalities at any time; and (b)

---

475 DHSSPS Press Release, 'Health Minister Simon Hamilton has today announced radical changes to the way health and social care in Northern Ireland is delivered,' 4 November 2015.

476 Department of Health, Social Services and Public Safety, 'Health and Social Care Reform and Transformation - Getting the Structures Right', Consultation Analysis Report, March 2016.

477 http://www.bbc.co.uk/news/uk-northern-ireland-35887746

478 https://www.health-ni.gov.uk/news/we-must-continue-drive-reform-health-and-social-care-services-oneill

479 Department of Health Press Release, 'O'Neill launches 10 year vision for Health & Social Care', 25 October 2016.

480 NIHRC Press Release, 'Human Rights Commission's Review of Termination of Pregnancy Law to begin', 15 June 2015.

pregnancies which are a consequence of sexual crime up to the date when the foetus becomes capable of existing independently of the mother.[481]

The Chief Commissioner commented:

> *The Human Rights Commission welcomes today's landmark ruling. In taking this case we sought to change the law so that women and girls in Northern Ireland have the choice of accessing a termination of pregnancy locally in circumstances of fatal foetal abnormalities, rape or incest, without being criminalised for doing so.*
>
> *We are pleased that today that the High Court has held that the current law is incompatible with human rights and has ruled in the Commission's favour.*[482]

The Attorney General and the Justice Minister both lodged appeals to the High Court's ruling in January 2016. The Commission also cross-appealed the decision and reintroduced all of the original grounds brought before the High Court. The Court of Appeal hearing took place in June 2016 and judgment was reserved.

In February 2016, a number of amendments were tabled to the Justice No.2 Bill to amend the law on abortion in cases of fatal foetal abnormalities, rape and incest. However, the NI Assembly voted against changing the legislation, thus failing to comply with the court judgment.

The Health Minister announced in March 2016 that he and the Justice Minister had agreed to proceed with creating an inter-departmental working group to make recommendation on how the issue on fatal foetal abnormalities could be addressed. The Working Group has sent its report to the Heath and Justice Ministers but has not been made public.[483] The former Justice Minister, David Ford, has also tabled a Private Members Bill with the Speakers Office on reform of the law surrounding fatal foetal abnormalities.[484]

In March 2016, a woman who bought drugs on the internet to induce a miscarriage was given a suspended prison sentence. It was reported that she had been unable to raise the funds to travel to England for a termination. A number of other criminal proceedings under the Offences Against the Person Act 1861 are currently before the courts.

On 12 July 2016, the UN CRC Committee published its concluding observations on the UK.[485] The Committee recommended that abortion be decriminalised in all circumstances and that legislation in NI be reviewed to ensure girls' access to safe abortion and post-abortion care services.

On 14 July 2016, the UN ICESCR Committee published its concluding observations on the UK.[486] The Committee recorded its concern that abortion was still criminalised in all circumstances in NI, save for where the life of the mother was in danger. The Committee noted that this could lead to unsafe abortions and discriminated against women from low income families who could not afford to travel to access termination services. The Committee recommended that NI legislation on abortion be amended to make it compatible with women's rights to health, life and dignity.

---

481   Ref HOR97402014, No. 125661/01.

482   NIHRC Press Release, 'Human Rights Commission welcomes historic termination of pregnancy ruling', 30th November 2015.

483   NI Assembly, Official Report: Fatal Foetal Abnormality: Working Group Report, Answer to questions AQO 499/16-21, 18 October 2016.

484   Belfast Telegraph, David Ford submits private member's bill to reform Northern Ireland abortion law in case of fatal foetal abnormalities, 19 October 2016.

485   UN Committee on the Rights of the Child, Concluding Observations on the Fifth Periodic Report of the United Kingdom of Great Britain and NI, CRC/C/GBR/CO/5, UN CRC, 12 July 2016.

486   UN Committee on Economic, Social and Cultural Rights, Concluding observations on the sixth periodic report of the United Kingdom of Great Britain and Northern Ireland E/C.12/GBR/CO/6, UN Economic and Social Council, 14 July 2016.

Mental capacity

The Mental Capacity (NI) Act 2016 received royal assent on 9 May 2016. The Act provides a single legislative framework governing situations where a decision needs to be made in relation to the care, treatment (for a physical or mental illness) or personal welfare of a person aged 16 or over, who lacks capacity to make the decision for themselves. The Act therefore continues to make provision for substitute decision making. An act done or decision made for or on behalf of a person lacking mental capacity must be done or made in their best interests. The 2016 Act section 3 states:

1. The decision-maker must not just consider but have special regard to (so far as they are reasonably ascertainable) (a) the person's past and present wishes and feelings (and, in particular, any relevant written statement made by him when he had capacity); (b) the beliefs and values that would be likely to influence his decision if he had capacity; and (c) the other factors that he would be likely to consider if he were able to do so;

2. The decision-maker must, in relation to any act that is being considered, have regard to whether failure to do the act is likely to result in harm to other persons with resulting harm to P.

During the passage of the Act the Commission collaborated in a research project within the Essex Autonomy Project assessing compliance of capacity legislation and proposals across the UK with the UNCRPD, Article 12.

The significance of the reference to 'special regard' within the assessment of best interests under the Act has been identified as a progressive element of the 2016 Act. In June 2016 the Essex Autonomy Project stated:

it will be crucial to monitor how the Act's pioneering use of the concept of "special regard" is operationalised and adjudicated. Insofar as this concept is applied in form of rebuttable presumption approach, as we shall argue that it can and should be, it will represent an important step forward in the construction of a CRPD-compliant capacity statute. …. Insofar as the principle of special regard is operationalised as a rebuttable presumption approach along the lines recommended above, we believe that it could satisfy the relevant requirements of Art. 12.4.[487]

The test for capacity laid down within the Act is decision specific, section 3 provides that a person lacks capacity 'if, at the material time, the person is unable to make a decision for himself or herself about the matter'. It further makes clear that 'it does not matter whether the impairment or disturbance is caused by a disorder or disability or otherwise than by a disorder or disability'. Again the Essex Autonomy Project has highlighted that de-linking incapacity from identified disorder or disability is a 'significant innovation' in ensuring compliance with the CRPD, Article 12.[488]

The Act is not yet commenced. Prior to the commencement of the Act, a Code of Practice and numerous Regulations must be developed. The Commission continues to work closely with officials in ensuring the effective implementation of the Act in a manner in line with the CRPD, Article 12.

The 2016 Act will introduce a presumption of capacity in all persons over the age of 16 only.[489] For under 16 year olds the Department for Health, Social Service and Public Safety (now Department of Health) had committed to review how the current legal framework, principally the Children (NI) Order 1995, reflects the emerging capacity of children in a health and welfare context. In its previous annual statement the Commission advised that a project plan with a clearly defined timetable for this project

487 Essex Autonomy Project, 'Towards Compliance with CRPD Art. 12 in Capacity/Incapacity Legislation across the UK', June 2016
488 Essex Autonomy Project, 'Towards Compliance with CRPD Art. 12 in Capacity/Incapacity Legislation across the UK', June 2016, p. 21.
489 NIHRC, 'The 2013 Annual Statement: Human Rights in NI', 2013, p. 45.

should be developed and made publicly available.[490] However, during the Second Stage debate on the Bill the Minister for Health stated that there are 'simply no available resources and arguably no time to undertake such a wide-ranging project at this moment'.[491] In 2016 the UNCRC Committee raised concern that:

> *Children under the age of 16 years are excluded from the protection under the Mental Capacity Act (2005) in England and Wales, as well as under the Mental Capacity Act (2016) in Northern Ireland, including with regard to medical treatment without consent.*[492]

The UN CRC Committee further recommended that the State Party:

> *Review current legislation on mental health to ensure that the best interests and the views of the child are taken duly into account in cases of mental health treatment of children below the age of 16, in particular with regard to hospitalization and treatment without consent.*[493]

Access to healthcare for irregular migrants

In March 2015, new regulations on access to primary and secondary healthcare for migrants came into operation.[494] These regulations will ensure that all asylum seekers, and other specified migrant groups, have access to free healthcare while they are living in NI.[495] The regulations make provision, inter alia, for treatment in respect of infection for any Human Immunodeficiency Virus. Officials informed the Committee for Health, Social Services and Public Safety that the policy intention is that the regulations provide an exemption from charge for full treatment, bringing NI into line with the rest of the UK.[496]

In order to reflect the changes to the new regulations, Department of Health, Social Services and Public Safety (now Department of Health) has also amended the General Medical Services Regulations so that any visitor exempt from charges is able to access GP services. The aim of the amendments is to ensure that a person not ordinarily resident accesses healthcare at the most appropriate setting.[497]

The Commission remains concerned that there is still a potential gap in respect of undocumented or irregular migrants and their children who are not entitled to primary and secondary healthcare under the Regulation.[498] The Commission's research paper of 2011 recommended that an amendment or policy direction may be required to ensure that the full set of GP services, including access to a GP list (subject to discretion) is genuinely available to any persons.[499]

In its 2016 submission to the UN ICESCR Committee the Commission expressed concern that there are practical barriers impeding refused asylum seekers accessing healthcare. For example, the Commission has received reports that although refused asylum seekers are entitled, there are difficulties in getting to health care appointments because support provided by government

---

490 NIHRC, 'Submission to the Consultation on Proposals for New Mental Capacity Legislation for NI', September 2014, para 90.

491 NI Assembly, Official Report: Tuesday 16 June 2015.

492 UN Committee on the Rights of the Child, Concluding Observations on the Fifth Periodic Report of the United Kingdom of Great Britain and NI, CRC/C/GBR/CO/5, UN CRC, 12 July 2016, para 59(g)

493 UN Committee on the Rights of the Child, Concluding Observations on the Fifth Periodic Report of the United Kingdom of Great Britain and NI, CRC/C/GBR/CO/5, UN CRC, 12 July 2016, para 60

494 Law Centre (NI), 'New Rules on Access to Healthcare for Migrants in Northern Ireland,' March 2015. The regulations revoke a number of regulations including: Provision of Health Services to Persons not Ordinarily Resident Regulations (Northern Ireland) 2005; Provision of Health Services to Persons not Ordinarily Resident (Amendment) Regulations (Northern Ireland) 2008; Regulation 3 of The Charges for Drugs and Appliances and Provision of Health Services to Persons not Ordinarily Resident (Amendment) Regulations (Northern Ireland) 2009 and Provision of Health Services to Persons not Ordinarily Resident (Amendment) Regulations (Northern Ireland) 2013.

495 Provision of Health Services to Persons not Ordinarily Resident Regulations (Northern Ireland) 2015, Regulation 4.

496 Committee for Health, Social Services and Public Safety, 'Official Report: Implementation of EU cross border health directive and overseas visitors policy', 27 November 2013.

497 The Health and Personal Social Services (General Medical Services Contracts) (Amendment) Regulations (Northern Ireland) 2015.

498 The Health and Personal Social Services (General Medical Services Contracts) (Amendment) Regulations (Northern Ireland) 2015, Regulation 2(1) (general health services).

499 NIHRC, 'Access Denied or Paying When You Shouldn't. Access to publicly funded medical care, residency, visitors and non-British/Irish Citizens', 2011, p. 49.

(section 4 support) is voucher only support. This means for example, no cash to pay for transport to appointments. The Commission has also received reports of pregnant women not receiving section 4 support until quite late in their pregnancy, this has been due to delay in decision making and processing awards once the decision has been made. Again, transport is an issue; as section 4 support is given through a voucher so there is no cash to pay for transport to prenatal appointments.[500]

The UN ICESCR Committee expressed concern that refugees, asylum seekers and refused asylum seekers continue to face discrimination in accessing health-care services. The Committee noted that the Immigration Act 2014 had further restricted access to health services by temporary migrants and undocumented migrants. The Committee recommended that the State party take steps to ensure that temporary migrants and undocumented migrants, asylum seekers, refused asylum seekers, refugees have access to all necessary health-care services and reminds the State party that health facilities, goods and services should be accessible to everyone without discrimination, in line with article 12 of the Covenant.[501]

---

500 NIHRC, Submission to the UN Committee on Economic, Social and Cultural Rights on the 6th Periodic Report of the UK's compliance with ICESCR, April 2016, paras 49.1-49.5.

501 UN Committee on Economic, Social and Cultural Rights, Concluding observations on the sixth periodic report of the United Kingdom of Great Britain and Northern Ireland E/C.12/GBR/CO/6, UN Economic and Social Council, 14 July 2016, para 56.

Right to education

ICESCR	Article 13
CRC	Article 28
ECHR	Protocol 1, Article 2
CFREU	Article 14
CRPD	Article 24

Integrated education

In its 2008 concluding observations the UN CRC Committee expressed concern regarding 'the problem of segregation of education' in NI and recommended that measures be taken to address this.[502] The UN CRC Committee had previously noted the low percentage of schools that were integrated and recommended the NI Executive:

> increase the budget for and take appropriate measures and incentives to facilitate the establishment of additional integrated schools in Northern Ireland to meet the demand of a significant number of parents.[503]

In 2014/15, seven percent of pupils in NI attended an integrated school with the most common approach to achieving integrated status now being the transformation of existing schools.[504] There have been no new integrated schools established since 2008. In examining the relatively slow growth of integrated schooling despite the statutory obligation on the Department of Education NI to 'encourage and facilitate the development of integrated education'[505] the impact of the Department of Education NI planning policy has been identified as potentially creating barriers to the growth of integrated education.[506]

In a judicial review in 2013, an integrated school argued that the Department of Education NI 'area-based' approach to planning, which restricts growth for schools located near schools in other sectors that are struggling to fill all their available places, denied them the opportunity to expand in order to meet the high demand from parents for integrated places. The judgment found that the Department of Education NI must reconcile the need to strategically plan for the most appropriate growth of the schools' estate as a whole with their obligation under Article 64 of the Education Reform Order to facilitate the growth of the integrated sector:

> Using an analytical tool to plan for an area is of course acceptable and necessary, however the inflexibility of the projections used will have the effect of making it difficult to accommodate the A64 duty in future day to day decisions. The department need to be alive to the A64 duty at all levels, including the strategic level.[507]

502 UN Committee on the Rights of the Child, Concluding observations on the third and fourth Period Reports of the United Kingdom of Great Britain and Northern Ireland, CRC/C/GBR/CO/4, UN CRC, October 2008, para 66.

503 UN Committee on the Rights of the Child, Thirty-first session Consideration of Reports submitted by State Parties under Article 44 of the Convention, Concluding observations: United Kingdom of Great Britain and Northern Ireland CRC/C/15/Add.188, UN CRC, 9 October 2002, para 48.

504 Department of Education Website, 'Integrated Schools'. https://www.education-ni.gov.uk/articles/integrated-schools

505 Education Reform Order (NI) 1989, art. 64.

506 NI Executive Press Release, 'Review of integrated education gets underway', 27 January 2016.

507 Drumragh Integrated College's Application [2014] NIQB 69.

In 2015 the NI Assembly Committee for Education reported on its inquiry into the shared and integrated education recommending that the Department of Education NI revise its approach to planning for the development of new schools:

to recognise the increasingly diverse school population and changes to traditional designations and so as to promote increased mixing in schools.[508]

The Education Committee recommended that the Department of Education NI:

should accept the shortcomings of the Needs Model and revise it so as to recognise the increasingly diverse school population and changes to traditional designations and so as to promote increased mixing in schools.[509]

In January 2016 the Minister of Education announced a review of the planning, growth and development of integrated education. In announcing the review the Minister acknowledged that: 'Overall growth of the number of schools with an integrated management type has slowed since 2000 … [despite]… a high parental demand/support for integrated education'.[510] The Review team will: 'develop short and medium term proposals to develop a more integrated education system based on current legislation, enhance the network of viable schools and are cost effective and value for money'.[511] The Independent Review Panel has been undertaking a strategic assessment of the current arrangements for the planning and development of integrated education.

In May 2016 the UN CRC recommended that the State Party including the NI Executive:

actively promote a fully integrated education system.[512]

Shared education

The Shared Education Act (NI) 2016 received royal assent on 9 May 2016.

This Act places an obligation on the Department of Education NI to promote: 'shared education', which is defined in the Act as 'the education together of—(a) those of different religious belief, including reasonable numbers of both Protestant and Roman Catholic children or young persons; and (b) those who are experiencing socio-economic deprivation and those who are not, which is secured by the working together and co-operation of two or more relevant providers'.

The Act places an obligation on the Department to report on the impact of shared education on good relations between participating children and young people and on their attitudes towards persons from backgrounds other than their own.[513] The Commission welcomed the Act and the reporting obligations on the Department. The delivery of obligations contained within the Act will go some way towards ending segregation in schools. In September 2016 the Minister of Education announced:

Shared Education is now well established across Northern Ireland with approximately 134 partnerships involving 314 schools who have successfully applied for funding and are now actively engaged in the Programme. Opening another call for funding will help to further embed the good practice and learning which is already established to deliver improved outcomes for our children, young people and wider society.[514]

---

508   NI Assembly Committee for Education, 'Report on the Inquiry into Shared and Integrated', Education Reference: NIA 194/11-16, 1st July 2015.

509   NI Assembly Committee for Education, 'Position Paper: Area Based Planning', 1 June 2015.

510   Department of Education Press Release, 'Independent Review Panel calls on public to have say on integrated education' 24 March 2016

511   Department of Education Press Release, 'Review of integrated education gets underway' 27 January 2016

512   UN Committee on the Rights of the Child, Concluding Observations on the Fifth Periodic Report of the United Kingdom of Great Britain and NI, CRC/C/GBR/CO/5, UN CRC, 12 July 2016, para 72(e).

513   Ibid Clause 7.

514   NI Executive, 'Further opportunity to access £25million fund for Shared Education', 19 September 2016.

In 2016 the UN CRC recommended that the State party:

carefully monitor the provision of shared education, with the participation of children, in order to ensure that it facilitates social integration. [515]

In addition the UN ICESCR Committee recommended:

that the State party take all necessary measures to reduce the attainment gaps, particularly among children belonging to low-income families, including by reconsidering the austerity programmes adopted and effectively implementing measures aimed at reducing de facto discrimination and segregation of students based on their religion, national or social origin, as well as their economic background. [516]

Academic selection

In its 2008 concluding observations the UN CRC Committee recommended that the UK Government and devolved administration:

Put an end to the two-tier culture in NI by abolishing the 11+ transfer test and ensure that all children are included in admission arrangements in post-primary schools. [517]

In 2016 the Commission advised the UN CRC Committee that the Department of Education has abolished the 11+ transfer test and the last official transfer test took place in November 2008.[518] However, due to a lack of consensus within the NI Executive the then Minister of Education was unable to bring forward proposals for a non-selective system of school admission. The Commission further advised that research shows the use of privately funded tutoring is extremely prevalent and that the current situation has contributed towards children from poor socio-economic backgrounds under performing and the two tier system of education therefore continues.[519]

In 2016 the UN CRC Committee recommended that the State Party:

abolish the practice of unregulated admission tests to post-primary education in NI. [520]

In commenting on this concluding observation the current Minister of Education Peter Weir MLA stated:

I am committed to respecting and progressing the rights of children and young people and it is important that a collective approach across Executive Departments is taken when considering UN CRC Committee recommendations.

On the issue of selection, I have made it clear that I support the right of schools to select on the basis of academic ability. I will be discussing this issue with a wide range of stakeholders and will want to consider very carefully how any changes might be taken forward. [521]

In September 2016 the Minister of Education issued revised guidance entitled, 'The Procedure for Transfer from Primary to Post-primary Education'. The guidance endorses the use of academic

---

515 UN Committee on the Rights of the Child, Concluding Observations on the Fifth Periodic Report of the United Kingdom of Great Britain and NI, CRC/C/GBR/CO/5, UN CRC, 12 July 2016, para 73.

516 UN Committee on the Rights of the Child, Concluding Observations on the Fifth Periodic Report of the United Kingdom of Great Britain and NI, CRC/C/GBR/CO/5, UN CRC, 12 July 2016, para 57.

517 UN Committee on the Rights of the Child, Concluding observations on the third and fourth Period Reports of the United Kingdom of Great Britain and Northern Ireland, CRC/C/GBR/CO/4, UN CRC, October 2008, para 67.

518 NIHRC, 'Submission to the UN Committee on the Rights of the Child on the United Kingdom's Fifth Periodic Report on compliance with the UN Convention on the Rights of the Child', July 2015, paras 6.1 – 6.2.

519 'What do we know? Educational Opportunities and Outcomes'. Available at: www.ark.ac.uk/publications/books/fio/10_fio-education.pdf

520 UN Committee on the Rights of the Child, Concluding Observations on the Fifth Periodic Report of the United Kingdom of Great Britain and NI, CRC/C/GBR/CO/5, UN CRC, 12 July 2016, para 72(a).

521 AQW 1175/16-21 14/06/2016.

selection.[522] In correspondence to the Commission, the Minister has indicated that he supports, 'the right of schools to select on the basis of academic ability'. The guidance sets out how primary schools may help children prepare for admissions tests. Furthermore in October 2016 the Minister of Education announced the appointment of Professor Peter Tymms, from the school of education at Durham University, to work with the Association of Quality Education and the Post-Primary Transfer Consortium in the development of a common post-primary assessment for the purposes of academic selection. However the Minister has stated that a 'state transfer test' would not be introduced.[523]

Educational needs of Traveller children

In November 2013 the Minister of Education for NI published the Traveller Child in Education Action Framework, at the launch of the Framework the Minister stated:

This is very much a Framework for action. It is the start of the journey of inclusion, to ensure that Traveller children have the opportunity to benefit from the educational opportunities on offer [the Minister further stated] An independent Monitoring and Evaluation Group will be established within the next few months to monitor the Action Framework. That group will report progress directly to me.[524]

In January 2016 in responding to a written question the then Minister stated that: 'The Traveller Education Monitoring Group has not yet been established'.[525] This remains the position. The absence of a Monitoring Group is a significant obstacle to assessing the effectiveness of the Framework.

In its 2016 concluding observations the UN CRC Committee raised concerns that:

(a) Substantial inequalities persist in educational attainment, particularly for boys, children living in poverty, Roma, gypsy and traveller children, children with disabilities, children in care and newcomer children;

(b) Among children subject to permanent or temporary school exclusions, there is a disproportionate number of boys, Roma, gypsy and traveller children, children of Caribbean descent, children living in poverty and children with disabilities.[526]

Special educational needs

The NI Executive is required by the CRPD, Article 24, to ensure that children with intellectual impairments have access to an inclusive education system.[527]

In 2016 the UN CRC Committee noted:

Many children with disabilities are still placed in special schools or special units in mainstream schools and many school buildings and facilities are not made fully accessible to children with disabilities;

With reference to its general comment No. 9 (2006) on the rights of children with disabilities, the Committee recommends that the State party adopt a human rights-based approach to disability, set up a comprehensive strategy for the inclusion of children with disabilities and set up comprehensive measures to further develop inclusive education, ensure that inclusive

---

522 Department of Education, 'The Procedure for Transfer From Primary to Post-Primary Education', Circular Number 2016/15, 7th September 2016.

523 BBC News NI, 'Department seeks single transfer test by 2017', 31 October 2016.

524 NI Executive Press Release, 'Traveller children and young people should be encouraged to value education and supported to reach their full potential', Wednesday 13 November 2013.

525 AQW 53269/11-16.

526 UN Committee on the Rights of the Child, Concluding Observations on the Fifth Periodic Report of the United Kingdom of Great Britain and NI, CRC/C/GBR/CO/5, UN CRC, 12 July 2016, para 71

527 In addition see, UN Committee on the Rights of the Child, General Comment No. 9 (2006) The rights of children with disabilities CRC/C/GC/9/Corr.1, UN CRC, 13 November 2007, para 66.

education is given priority over the placement of children in specialized institutions and classes and make mainstream schools fully accessible to children with disabilities.[528]

The Special Educational Needs and Disability (NI) Act 2016 received royal assent in March 2016. Throughout the year, the Department of Education has consulted on Regulations required to operationalise the new legislation. The Commission has highlighted the recommendations of the UN CRC Committee relating to special educational needs and continues to advise of the need to ensure no retrogression in the enjoyment of the right to education for children with disabilities.[529] The Commission has also highlighted that provision for the piloting of appeal rights for children under 16 should be operationalised as soon as possible, in line with the UN CRC Committee's previous concluding observation.[530]

Bullying in Schools

The Minister for Education introduced the Addressing Bullying in Schools Bill to the Assembly at the end of 2015 with the purpose of creating a statutory definition of bullying where none had previously existed and creating duties around preventing bullying and recording bullying incidents for all grant-aided schools. The Addressing Bullying in Schools (NI) Act 2016 received royal assent on 12 May 2016.[531]

The Commission, in its evidence to the Education Committee during the scrutiny of this Bill, welcomed the progressive principles of the legislation and noted that taking measures to address bullying is in line with a number of human rights instruments including the ECHR, UNCRC and ICESCR.[532] The Commission also highlighted a range of instruments that require specific action to address violence directed towards particular groups such as persons with disabilities,[533] women and girls,[534] persons belonging to national minorities,[535] persons of different racial groups[536] and people of different sexual orientations and gender identities.[537]

The Commission welcomed the categories listed under the duty to record the motivation of bullying, address the majority of grounds for discrimination and vulnerable groups but also advised that bullying of young mothers constitutes a barrier to the full enjoyment of the right to education for women and girls.[538] The legislation was subsequently amended to include 'persons with dependents and persons without'. However, no changes were made to reflect the Commission's concerns that bullying also presents a significant barrier for linguistic minorities and children experiencing socio-economic deprivation. The legislation does enable the Department in section 3 (4) to amend the included

---

528 UN Committee on the Rights of the Child, Concluding Observations on the Fifth Periodic Report of the United Kingdom of Great Britain and NI, CRC/C/GBR/CO/5, UN CRC, 12 July 2016, para 56(b).

529 NIHRC, Response to the consultation on the SEND Bill (2015), para 27; See http://www.nihrc.org/uploads/publications/NIHRC_response_to_the_Consultation_on_the_SEND_Bill.pdf

530 UN Committee on the Rights of the Child, Concluding observations on the third and fourth Period Reports of the United Kingdom of Great Britain and Northern Ireland, CRC/C/GBR/CO/4, UN CRC, October 2008, paras 66-67.

531 Addressing Bullying in Schools Act (NI) 2016. Available at http://www.legislation.gov.uk/nia/2016/25

532 NIHRC, Submission on Addressing Bullying in Schools Bill, 2016. Available at http://www.nihrc.org/uploads/publications/NIHRC_submission_on_Addressing_Bullying_in_Schools_Bill_2016.pdf

533 Convention on the Rights of Persons with Disabilities, Article 24 requires the State to ensure an inclusive education system at all levels directed to 'The full development of human potential and sense of dignity and self-worth, and the strengthening of respect for human rights, fundamental freedoms and human diversity'.

534 Convention on the Elimination of All Forms of Discrimination against Women, Article 10 requires the State to take all appropriate measures to eliminate discrimination against women in the field of education.

535 Framework Convention for the Protection of National Minorities, Article 12 requires Parties to the Convention to undertake to promote equal opportunities for access to education at all levels for persons belonging to national minorities.

536 International Convention on the Elimination of All Forms of Racial Discrimination, Article 5 requires the State to prohibit and eliminate racial discrimination to guarantee the right to education. In it's 2016 Concluding Observations on the UK the CERD Committee noted concern at 'continued reports of racist bullying and harassment' and recommended that the State party 'strengthen efforts to eliminate it'. This should include data collection, developing concrete strategies, training staff and ensuring the curriculum contains accurate accounts of 'the history of the British Empire and colonialism'. See http://tbinternet.ohchr.org/Treaties/CERD/Shared%20Documents/GBR/CERD_C_GBR_CO_21-23_24985_E.pdf

537 The International Panel of Experts on International Human Rights Law and on Sexual Orientation and Gender Identity, The Yogyakarta Principles: Principles on the Application of International Human Rights Law in Relation to Sexual Orientation and Gender Identity, March 2007. The Principles provide that States shall 'Ensure that laws and policies provide adequate protection for students, staff and teachers of different sexual orientations and gender identities against all forms of social exclusion and violence within the school environment, including bullying and harassment.'

538 See Strategic objective B.1 (Ensure Equal Access to Education) Action 80g, http://www.un.org/womenwatch/daw/beijing/platform/educa.htm

grounds by Order subject to negative resolution. This provision could be engaged should evidence suggest that those groups identified by the Commission are being significantly targeted.

The Commission also advised that the State has a positive duty to secure the child's right to education regardless of whether they are in a private or public setting.[539] Therefore children should have statutory protection from bullying regardless of where the educational provision takes place. Since the duties to prevent bullying and record bullying incidents in the legislation apply only to 'grant aided schools' the Commission remains concerned about how bullying will be addressed in respect of the 14 independent schools in NI.

539   Kjeldsen, Busk Madsen and Pedersen v. Denmark, Application Nos. 5095/71, 5920/72, 5926/72, Judgement of 7 December 1976, para 50.

Right to participate in the cultural life of the community

ICCPR	Article 27
CRC	Article 31
ICESCR	Article 15
FCNM	Article 5
CEDAW	Article 13 (c)
CRPD	Article 30
CFREU	Article 13 Article 22
European Charter for Regional or Minority Languages	

The Irish language and Ulster Scots

The Commission has consistently highlighted the need to ensure adequate legal protection for the Irish language and for Ulster Scots. In 2012 the Commission reported that the Advisory Committee on the FCNM had identified the protection and promotion of the Irish language as requiring immediate action, recommending that the UK Government and NI Executive:

develop comprehensive legislation on the Irish language in NI and take resolute measures to protect and implement more effectively the language rights of persons belonging to the Irish speaking community.[540]

In 2012 the then Department of Culture Arts and Leisure issued separate consultation papers in respect of strategies to promote and enhance the Irish language and Ulster Scots.[541] Each consultation document referred to the UK's obligations under the Charter with respect to the Irish language and Ulster Scots. However, in 2013 the Commission reported that it had raised issues with the European Charter for Regional or Minority Languages Committee of Experts around continuing gaps in legislation, education needs and the responsibility of the NI Executive to promote and develop minority language protections i n NI.[542]

In 2014 Committee of Experts made recommendations relating to the compliance of the UK with the European Charter on Minority and Regional Languages.[543] In its report the Committee of Experts noted with regret that the NI Executive had not contributed to the State Report, the Committee further stated:

The devolution settlement in NI presents obstacles to the promotion and the protection of regional or minority languages to the extent that there is no political consensus on the contribution to be made by the NI Government. The responsibility of competence with regard to regional or minority languages was devolved to the NI Assembly. Nevertheless, no legislation

---

540 Advisory Committee on the Framework Convention for the Protection of National Minorities, Third Opinion on the United Kingdom adopted on 30 June 2011 ACFC/OP/III(2011)006, 22 December 2011, p. 43.

541 NIHRC, 'Annual Statement on Human Rights in NI 2012', December 2012, p. 39.

542 NIHRC, 'Annual Statement on Human Rights in NI 2013', December 2013, p. 48.

543 Council of Europe, 'Report of the Committee of Experts on the Charter Strasbourg,' 4th monitoring cycle, ECRML. (2014) 1, COMEX Application of the Charter in the UK, 15 January 2014.

promoting the Irish language has been adopted. The Committee of Experts was informed that this is because of the need to obtain consensus within the power sharing administration.[544]

The Committee of Experts urged:

the authorities to provide an appropriate legislative base for the protection and promotion of Irish in NI.[545]

In January 2015 the then Department of Culture Arts and Leisure published strategies on both the Irish language and Ulster Scots language.[546] The Department then consulted on proposals for an Irish Language Bill, the Commission welcomed the proposal to provide statutory protections for the Irish language.[547]

The then Department of Culture Arts and Leisure acknowledged that the Committee of Experts has specifically considered the Administration of Justice (Language) Act (Ireland) 1737 under Article 7(2), and in its third report stated that:

… the prohibition of the use of Irish in courts in Northern Ireland by the 1737 Act is an unjustified restriction relating to the use of Irish, endangering the development of the language.[548]

The Commission welcomed the proposed repeal of the Administration of Justice (Language) Act (Ireland) 1737 and highlighted the need to ensure that the use of Irish in the courts will be facilitated at an operational level.[549]

Whilst welcoming the proposal to place Irish medium education on a statutory footing the Commission noted a lack of detail within the consultation paper as to how this commitment will be realised.[550] The Commission highlighted that such a proposal would require the support and agreement of Department of Education NI. The Commission highlighted that to realise many of the proposals within the Bill would require cross departmental co-operation. Officials briefed the NI Assembly Culture, Arts and Leisure Committee in October 2015. Officials informed the Committee at that time of the intention to publish a report of the consultation in the near future. Officials indicated that the Minister remained committed to an Irish Language Act and to progress the Bill as far as possible and urged all sides of the house to support the Bill. The next stage was to bring policy proposals to the NI Executive for agreement.[551]

At the time of writing an Irish Language Bill has not been introduced to the NI Assembly. Responsibility for the Irish Language Bill now rests with the Department for Communities. The Commission updated the UN ICESCR Committee in 2015 and advised of the need to bring forward policy proposals for an Irish Language Act at the earliest opportunity.[552] In addition the Commission asked the UN ICESCR Committee to seek an update on the implementation of actions contained within the strategy on developing the Ulster Scots language, culture and heritage.[553]

---

544 Council of Europe, 'Report of the Committee of Experts on the Charter Strasbourg,' 4th monitoring cycle, ECRML. (2014) 1, COMEX Application of the Charter in the UK, 15 January 2014, paras 12-14.

545 Council of Europe, 'Report of the Committee of Experts on the Charter Strasbourg,' 4th monitoring cycle, ECRML. (2014) 1, COMEX Application of the Charter in the UK, 15 January 2014, paras 12-14.

546 Strategy to Enhance and Protect the Development of the Irish Language 2015-2035; Strategy to Enhance and Develop the Ulster-Scots Language, Heritage and Culture 2015-2035.

547 NIHRC, 'Response to the proposals for an Irish Language Bill', May 2015.

548 Council of Europe, 'Application of the Charter in the United Kingdom', 3rd Monitoring Cycle, Report of the Committee of Experts on the Charter Strasbourg, ECRML. (2010) 4, COMEX, 21 Apr 2010, para 121.

549 NIHRC, 'Response to the proposals for an Irish Language Bill', May 2015, para 34.

550 NIHRC, 'Response to the proposals for an Irish Language Bill', May 2015, para 66.

551 Information obtained from a recording of the meeting of the Culture, Arts and Leisure Committee on 1st October 2015.

552 NIHRC, 'Submission to the United Nations Committee on Economic, Social and Cultural Rights: Parallel Report on the Sixth Periodic Report of the UK under the International Covenant on Economic, Social and Cultural Rights', September 2015, p. 67.

553 NIHRC, 'Submission to the United Nations Committee on Economic, Social and Cultural Rights: Parallel Report on the Sixth Periodic Report of the UK under the International Covenant on Economic, Social and Cultural Rights', September 2015, p. 67.

In 2016 the ICESCR Committee noted its concern about the lack of effective measures adopted by the State party to promote the use of the Irish language in NI and reiterated its previous recommendation that the State party adopt an Irish language Act.[554]

In its 2016 submission to the Advisory Committee of the FCMN, the Commission advised the Committee to seek further information on the progress of the Irish Language Bill; measures being taken to overcome the politicization of the language; and, how it will fulfil its obligations to promote the Irish language in the absence of political consensus in NI.[555]

An Irish language organisation, Conradh na Gaeilge, has initiated judicial review proceedings against the NI Executive over its failure to adopt or implement an Irish language plan. The High Court granted leave in May 2016 and it is expected that the case will be heard in 2016.[556]

554 UN Committee on Economic, Social and Cultural Rights, Concluding observations on the sixth periodic report of the United Kingdom of Great Britain and Northern Ireland E/C.12/GBR/CO/6, UN Economic and Social Council, 14 July 2016, para 67 – 68

555 NIHRC, Submission to the Advisory Committee on the Framework Convention for the Protection of National Minorities: Parallel Report to the Advisory Committee on the Fourth Monitoring Report of the UK, 2016

556 Conradh na Gaeilge, Conradh na Gaeilge granted High Court's Permission to bring Judicial Review Proceedings against Executive, 31 May 2016.

Constitutional Protections

A Bill of Rights for NI

As required by the Belfast (Good Friday) Agreement and the NI Act 1998, the Commission provided advice to the UK Government on a Bill of Rights for NI in 2008. On receipt of its advice the NI Office sought views from the public by way of a public consultation.[557]

In December 2010 the then Minister of State within the NI Office reported that there was:

considerable support from human rights and community groups for a wide-ranging Bill of Rights along the lines of that recommended by the NI Human Rights Commission.[558]

Since 2010 it has been consistently stated by Government ministers that there has been a lack of political consensus around a Bill of Rights for NI.[559] The Commission has repeatedly reported on the absence of any significant development to progress a Bill of Rights for NI.

In 2016 the Commission updated the UN Committee for CRC on the lack of progress in relation to a Bill of Rights for NI. The Committee subsequently recommended that the State Party:

Expedite the enactment of a Bill of Rights for Northern Ireland, agreed under the Good Friday Agreement.[560]

The Commission also updated the UN Committee for ICESCR who noted 'that a bill of rights for Northern Ireland has not yet been adopted, as provided by the Belfast (Good Friday) Agreement'. The Committee's concluding observation stated:

the Committee recalls its previous recommendation (see E/C.12/GBR/CO/5, para. 10) and urges the State party to take all necessary measures to expedite the adoption of a bill of rights for Northern Ireland.[561]

A UK Bill of Rights

In October 2014 the Conservative Party issued a paper proposing the reform of human rights protections in the UK, including the repeal of the Human Rights Act 1998 and its replacement with a 'British Bill of Rights and Responsibilities'.[562] This aim was reflected in the Conservative party manifesto and in the Queen's Speech of May 2015. However, proposals were not published during 2015 and the issue was again included within the 2016 Queen's speech.[563]

In the 2015 Queen's speech the Government announced that it:

will bring forward proposals for a Bill of Rights to replace the Human Rights Act. This would reform and modernise our human rights legal framework and restore common sense to the application of human rights laws. It would also protect existing rights, which are an essential part of a modern, democratic society, and better protect against abuse of the system and misuse of human rights.[564]

557 NIO, 'Consultation Paper: A Bill of Rights for NI: Next Steps', November 2009.

558 Minister of State Hugo Swire MP, Written Ministerial Statement to Parliament, 16 December 2010.

559 Westminster Hall Tuesday 16 July 2013 [Mr Christopher Chope in the Chair] Column 190WH Bill of Rights (NI).

560 UN Committee on the Rights of the Child, Concluding Observations on the Fifth Periodic Report of the United Kingdom of Great Britain and NI, CRC/C/GBR/CO/5, UN CRC, 12 July 2016, para 9.

561 UN Committee on Economic, Social and Cultural Rights, Concluding observations on the sixth periodic report of the United Kingdom of Great Britain and Northern Ireland E/C.12/GBR/CO/6, UN Economic and Social Council, 14 July 2016, para 10.

562 Conservative Party, Protecting Human Rights in the UK: The Conservatives' Proposals for Changing Britain's Human Rights Laws, 2014.

563 Cabinet Office, 'Queen's Speech 2016', 18 May 2016.

564 Queen's Speech Briefing Pack, 27 May 2015. https://www.gov.uk/government/uploads/system/uploads/attachment_data/file/430149/QS_lobby_pack_FINAL_NEW_2.pdf

The 2016 Queen's speech stated that:

Proposals will be brought forward for a British Bill of Rights.[565] *The new Lord Chancellor has confirmed the Government's intention remains to bring forward proposals, although a timetable has not been provided.*[566] *The Government has confirmed that it is not Government policy to leave the Council of Europe.*[567]

Speaking following a visit to the UK, Nils Muižnieks, the Council of Europe Commissioner for Human Rights stated:

The repeatedly delayed launch of the consultation process for repeal of the Human Rights Act has created much speculation and an atmosphere of anxiety and concern in civil society and in some parts of the devolved administrations. There is a real fear of regression in terms of rights' protection in the United Kingdom.[568]

In 2016 the UN ICESCR Committee recommended:

that the State party undertake a broad public consultation on its plan to repeal the Human Rights Act 1998 as well as on the proposal for a new bill of rights. It also recommends that the State party take all necessary measures to ensure that any new legislation in this regard is aimed at enhancing the status of human rights, including economic, social and cultural rights, in the domestic legal order and that it provide effective protection of those rights across all jurisdictions of the State party.[569]

A Charter of Rights for the island of Ireland

The Commission and the Irish Human Rights Commission were mandated by the Belfast (Good Friday) Agreement 1998 to consider through a joint committee:

the possibility of establishing a charter, open to signature by all democratic political parties, reflecting and endorsing agreed measures for the protection of the fundamental rights of everyone living in the island of Ireland.[570]

This task was completed in June 2011 when the Commissions' together presented advice to the Governments of the UK and Ireland, the Speaker of the NI Assembly and the Ceann Comhairle of Dáil Éireann.[571] The Speaker and Ceann Comhairle both agreed to forward the advice to political parties in their respective legislative bodies for further consideration. Since then no further communication has been received on this matter.

In June 2015 both Commissions' made a presentation to the Joint Oireachtas Committee on the Implementation of the Good Friday/Belfast Agreement.[572] In its presentation to the Committee, the Commissions referred to the establishment of the North-South Parliamentary Forum and the potential for the Charter to form part of its work plan as part of an active consideration on the establishment of a Charter of Rights for the island of Ireland. However, no further developments have occurred in 2016.

565 Cabinet Office, 'Queen's Speech 2016', 18 May 2016.

566 House of Commons Justice Committee, Oral evidence: The work of the Secretary of State, HC 620, Wednesday 7 September 2016.

567 House of Commons Vol. 611, Column 1615, 14 June 2016. https://hansard.parliament.uk/Commons/2016-06-14/debates/16061428000011/EUMembershipHumanRights

568 Council of Europe, 'UK: Forthcoming reforms to human rights law must not weaken protection', 22 January 2016. http://www.coe.int/rm/web/commissioner/view/-/asset_publisher/ugj3i6qSEkhZ/content/uk-forthcoming-reforms-to-human-rights-law-must-not-weaken-protection?_101_INSTANCE_ugj3i6qSEkhZ_languageId=en_GB

569 UN Committee on Economic, Social and Cultural Rights, Concluding observations of the Committee on Economic, Social and Cultural Rights on the fourth to fifth Periodic Reports of the United Kingdom of Great Britain and Northern Ireland, E/C.12/GBR/CO/5, UN Economic and Social Council, June 2009.

570 The Joint Committee of the NIHRC and the Irish Human Rights Commission, 'The advice of the joint committee on a charter of rights for the island of Ireland', June 2011.

571 See http://www.nihrc.org/publication/category/Charter-of-Rights

572 Joint Statement, IHREC and NIHRC, 25 June 2015. Available at: http://www.nihrc.org/news/detail/joint-statement-of-irish-human-rights-and-equality-commission-and-northern

National human rights institution

Recent amendments to the NI Act 1998 provide that the functions of the Secretary of State for NI relating to the Commission may be transferred to the competency of the NI Assembly through an Order of Parliament.[573] No such Order has been laid in 2016.

Prior to the laying of such an Order the Secretary of State must provide a report to the Houses of Parliament relating to the potential implications of a transfer on the effectiveness and independence of the Commission.[574] The Commission remains of the view that any transfer of the responsibilities of the Secretary of State should be to the NI Assembly, in line with the Belgrade Principles.

In 2009/2010, the NIHRC's cash budget was £1,702,000. The NIHRC's budget for 2016/17 is to be £1,149,000 and this is to decrease by £25,000 each year until 2019-20, when the budget is planned to be £1,075,000.[575] The Commission raised concerns regarding its funding with the UN Human Rights Committee.[576] The Committee recommended that:

The State party should provide the Northern Ireland Human Rights Commission with adequate funding to enable it to discharge its mandate effectively and independently, in full compliance with the Paris Principles (General Assembly resolution 48/134, annex).[577]

The Commission's accreditation as an A status NHRI was subject to its five year review by the Global Alliance of National Institutions for the Promotion and Protection of Human Rights in May 2016 as required by the UN and it was successfully re-awarded A status.[578] It was noted that the Commission had experienced a significant cut in its budget since 2009 and that this will continue until 2019. The Commission was encouraged to advocate for an appropriate level of funding to effectively carry out its mandate and to advocate for amendments to its enabling law to allow it to receive donor funding without prior government approval.

UK membership of the European Union

A referendum on whether the UK should leave or remain in the European Union took place on Thursday 23 June 2016. Of the voting public 51.9 percent voted to leave and 48.1 percent voted to remain. The referendum turnout was 71.8 percent, with more than 30 million people voting. In NI, however, 55.8% voted remain and 44.2% voted to leave the European Union

For the UK to leave the European Union it has to invoke Article 50 of the Treaty of the European Union introduced through the Lisbon Treaty. The Prime Minister, Theresa May has confirmed this will be done by spring of 2017, meaning the UK is expected to have left by 2019, depending on the timetable agreed during negotiations. Under Article 50, the European Union Treaties shall cease to apply two years after the UK gives official notification that it wants to leave. The European Council must obtain the consent of the European Parliament before concluding a withdrawal agreement by way of a 'super qualified majority' vote (72 percent of the members of the Council, comprising at least 65 percent of the European Union population). Legislation that implements European Union Directives in the UK will remain in force until they are amended or repealed by Parliament, but European Union Regulations may no longer apply.[579] In October 2016 the Prime Minister, Theresa May MP indicated her intention

---

573 NI (Miscellaneous Provisions) Act 2014.

574 NIHRC, 'The 2013 Annual Statement: Human Rights in NI', December 2013, p. 50.

575 This reduction is significantly less that the 40% cuts applied to some other government departments. However, over the past ten years, this amounts to an overall percentage reduction of 36.8%.

576 NIHRC, 'Submissions to the UN Human Rights Committee on the UK's Seventh Periodic Report on compliance with the ICCPR', May 2015, para 2.6.

577 UN Human Rights Committee, Concluding observations on the seventh periodic report of the United Kingdom of Great Britain and Northern Ireland, CCPR/C/GBR/CO/7, UN HRC, July 2015, para 7.

578 GANHRI, Report and Recommendations of the Session of the Sub-Committee on Accreditation, 9-13 MAY 2016, pp. 46-47.

579 Paul Bowers, Arabella Lang, Vaughne Miller, Ben Smith, Dominic Webb, 'Brexit: some legal and constitutional issues and alternatives to EU membership', House of Commons Library, 28 July 2016. p. 49.

to bring forward a 'Great Repeal Act' to repeal the European Communities Act of 1972 and bring an end to the primacy of European Union law within the UK.[580]

The impact of a UK exit from the European Union is uncertain and the effect on the human rights protections introduced to UK law by virtue of membership in the European Union is also unclear. A House of Commons Research and Library service briefing paper summarised the current position in the following terms:

> *If the UK withdrew from the European Union, it would no longer have to comply with the human rights obligations of the European Union Treaties, including with the Charter of Fundamental Rights of the European Union (CFREU). Although the CFREU was not intended to create any new rights, a breach can result in the UK courts disapplying UK Acts of Parliament – something they cannot do under other human rights instruments.[581]*

The CRFEU replicates many of the civil and political rights contained within the ECHR and goes beyond them in providing protection for the right to the protection of personal data and to dignity and for a number of socio-economic rights.

The Commission provided a briefing to the UN ICESCR Committee in advance on the referendum advising the Committee to recommend that: all necessary steps are taken so that there is no detriment to all current rights and benefits for UK citizens and European Union nationals residing in the UK in relation to employment, social security, health care and public services in the European Union, notwithstanding the outcome of the referendum.[582]

In October 2016 the Commission made a submission to an inquiry by the Joint Committee of Human Rights on the human rights implications of EU withdrawal. In its submission the Commission highlighted the potential implication of withdrawal from the EU on freedom of movement for persons living close to the border with Ireland.[583]

In October 2016 two applications for judicial review relating to the process of withdrawal were rejected by the NI High Court.[584] However on 3 November 2016 the High Court in England & Wales ruled that:

> *The Secretary of State [for Exiting the European Union] does not have the power under the Crown's prerogative to give notice pursuant to Article 50 of the Treaty of Europe for the UK to withdraw from the European Union.[585]*

The High Court decision has been appealed and the full Supreme Court of eleven judges will hear the the appeal in December 2016. The Supreme Court will also hear an appeal from the applicants who were before the NI High Court.

HM Government depending on the outcome may have to seek the approval of HM Parliament before giving notice of withdrawal as required by Article 50 of the Treaty of Europe.

---

580 BBC News, 'Brexit: Theresa May to trigger Article 50 by end of March', 2 October 2016.

581 Vaughne Miller, 'Brexit: impact across policy areas', House of Commons Library, 26 August 2016, para 13.1.

582 NIHRC, Submission to the UN Committee on Economic, Social and Cultural Rights 58th Session on the Sixth Periodic Report of the United Kingdom's Compliance with ICESCR, 2016.

583 NIHRC, Submission to JCHR Inquiry - What are the human rights implications of Brexit inquiry?, October 2016

584 McCord's (Raymond) Application [2016] NIQB 85.

585 R (Miller) -V- Secretary of State for Exiting the European Union [2016] EWHC 2768 (Admin)